"If you're looking to save time while also crafting food that is healthy, flavorful, and creative, look no further than this essential resource. With *Vegan Pressure Cooking*, JL Fields has crafted that rarest of things: a cookbook that is beautiful and practical at once. The recipes are highly accessible and easy to prepare, and you'll be immediately drawn in by her personable voice and culinary savvy."
–Gena Hamshaw, C.C.N., author of *Choosing Raw*

"A collection of thrillingly easy-to-make, yet scrumptious, recipes that get you to be best buddies with a pressure cooker. JL takes the fear out of cooking under pressure and puts fun and finesse into humble beans, grains, and veggies, turning them into everything from delectable one-pot dishes to desserts."
–Miyoko Schinner, author of *Artisan Vegan Cheese*, and others
(www.artisanveganlife.com)

"In this beautiful and accessible book, the irrepressible JL Fields reinvents 'fast' food healthfully, deliciously, and passionately. And she proves beyond a doubt that this is not your grandma's pressure cooking."
–Victoria Moran, author of *Main Street Vegan* and
director of Main Street Vegan Academy
(www.mainstreetvegan.net)

"*Vegan Pressure Cooking* is full of creative, kind, and delicious recipes that'll inspire you to get back into the kitchen tonight!"
–Annie Shannon, co-author of *Betty Goes Vegan*

# VEGAN
## PRESSURE COOKING

### DELICIOUS BEANS, GRAINS *and* ONE-POT MEALS IN MINUTES

JL FIELDS

**Fair Winds Press**
100 Cummings Center, Suite 406L
Beverly, MA 01915

fairwindspress.com • quarryspoon.com

© 2015 Fair Winds Press
Photography © Kate Lewis Photography

First published in the USA in 2015 by
Fair Winds Press, a member of
Quarto Publishing Group USA Inc.
100 Cummings Center
Suite 406-L
Beverly, MA 01915-6101
www.fairwindspress.com

19 18 17 16 15     1 2 3 4 5

ISBN: 978-1-59233-644-9

Digital edition published in 2015
eISBN: 978-1-62788-188-3

Library of Congress Cataloging-in-Publication Data available

Book and cover design by Amanda Richmond

Printed and bound in China

The information in this book is for educational purposes only. It is not
intended to replace the advice of a physician or medical practitioner.
Please see your health care provider before beginning any new health program.

To Janice and Larry Fields,
for instilling in me a desire to try
to make life better for every living being.

To Dave Burgess,
for loving me for who I was,
who I am, and who I will be.

This book is because of you three.

# Contents

# Introduction

I hold three people responsible for my pressure-cooking obsession—authors Gena Hamshaw, Lorna Sass, and Jill Nussinow. Four years ago, after eight years as a vegetarian, I went vegan. During that first year as a new vegan, I made a point to read vegan blogs, plant-based cookbooks, and nutrition books. I wanted to get it right, this vegan thing, and after years of counting on my husband to do most of the cooking, I felt like a fish out of water. So when one of my favorite bloggers, Gena Hamshaw of *Choosing Raw*, wrote a compelling, convincing post about the virtues of the pressure cooker—especially for vegans—I was sold. I ordered my first pressure cooker and the cookbook *Great Vegetarian Cooking Under Pressure* by Lorna Sass, and my obsession began.

Not long after learning how to use my pressure cooker, I began to chronicle my adventures (and misadventures) on my blog, JL Goes Vegan. Cookbook author Jill Nussinow reached out to help me along the way. She event wrote a terrific "Pressure Cooker 101" post for my blog, and I began turning to her books religiously. To this day, Jill and I are comrades in pressure cooker activism in and out of the vegan community.

I am not a trained chef. I am a home cook. I simply took the initiative to sign up for a few public education courses at culinary schools to learn how to get more creative in the kitchen and cook intuitively. My recipes are wholesome and delicious and have been developed to demonstrate how easy it is to cook and eat a well-balanced plant-based diet, even if you consider yourself a busy non-cook—actually, *especially* if you consider yourself a busy non-cook.

As a vegan lifestyle coach and educator, I work primarily with clients who are not necessarily inclined to go vegan but are highly motivated to live more healthfully by eating a whole-foods, plant-based diet. I realize that not everyone reading this book is vegan or plans to go vegan. Many people want to learn how to incorporate more plants into their diet to improve their health or to have a more positive impact on the environment. And, of course, there are vegans who want to avoid using or consuming animals. Wherever you are on the veg-spectrum, I want to help. I teach cooking classes and demonstrate how accessible—and essential—the pressure cooker is when following a plant-based diet. I believe that using a pressure cooker will get you back into your kitchen. You will get excited about making dried beans from scratch and getting creative with grains the likes of which you may have never considered cooking or eating.

In this book I will provide you with tips, tricks, and techniques—and delicious, easy recipes—that will help you use the pressure cooker to incorporate more vegetables, legumes and beans, and grains into your diet quickly and easily. Who's ready to have some fun?

**CHAPTER ONE**

# Pressure Cooking 101

Why use a pressure cooker? Simply put, this nifty, no-frills appliance helps you make beans and grains—and, in turn, *meals*—in minutes. Sure, you can buy canned beans or instant rice, but once you realize how quickly you can prepare home-cooked beans and grains, I don't think you'll want to. How *quickly*, you ask?

- Quinoa: 1 minute
- Bulgur: 5 minutes
- Black-eyed peas: 6 minutes
- Brown lentils: 8 minutes

- Adzuki beans: 9 minutes
- Chickpeas: 15 minutes
- Pearl barley: 18 minutes
- Brown rice: 22 minutes

You can also save money. In a cost-per-serving analysis of dried beans versus canned beans, you save roughly twice as much by purchasing dried and cooking them on your own. And you save a lot of sodium too, as the canned versions are often full of salt!

Aside from staples, the pressure cooker is, of course, great for one-pot meals: stews, soups, and more—as this book will show you! For an easy, healthy, filling dinner, I heat onions and garlic in a little olive oil in the pressure cooker and then mix and match vegetables and beans. Another quick and filling meal I love is based around cubed or small potatoes, which cook up in about 6 minutes in the pressure cooker. I cook the potatoes with packaged seitan or tofu, carrots and celery, maybe a diced tomato or two, and enough vegetable broth to cover everything. Six minutes under pressure and I am enjoying a hearty stew alongside a raw salad or sautéed greens.

Now that we know how a pressure cooker can save you time and money—and help you prepare healthy, nutritious, plant-based meals—let's talk about how easy it is to use a pressure cooker. Most people avoid using a pressure cooker because they are afraid of it or it feels too complicated, so let's get all of those pesky fears, apprehensions, and questions out of the way, shall we? I've taken your questions head-on. Let's get started!

"I most of all want to thank you for introducing me to a form of cooking that previously was totally intimidating to me. When I tell people I am pressure cooking I get the same response from each one of them: 'My mother had one but I'm too afraid of it.' And my answer to them is always the same: 'If I can do it, you can do it!' My pressure cooker is now a permanent fixture on my stove top, and I plan on happily using it carefree for many years to come."

—Barbara Ravid, recipe tester

# Your Common Questions, Answered

One of the reasons people avoid pressure cooking is because it seems alien to them—there are way too many questions and it feels complicated—so they avoid using one. But I assure you, it's just like any other appliance—and once I've answered your questions, you'll be ready to roll!

## HOW DO PRESSURE COOKERS WORK?

When cooking traditionally on the stove top, heat rises to 212°F (100°C) and liquid evaporates. When pressure cooking, you lock the lid in place, bring the liquid to a boil, and the heat rises to 250°F (121°C) while retaining all of the steam that would have normally evaporated—this allows for quicker cooking times as well as keeping all those good flavors in, instead of letting them out.

## HOW CAN I AVOID BLOWING UP MY PRESSURE COOKER?

I teach pressure cooking classes and this is almost everyone's fear—"the thing's going to blow!" This is highly unlikely, especially these days, with modern-day cookers carrying enough safety features in place to prevent this from happening altogether. That said, be sure to read the owner's manual for the specific safety precautions to follow for your device. In general, these include checking the vent pipe, cover lock, and seal for proper functioning and avoiding filling the pressure cooker beyond the "maximum" line. Some models also advise against using certain foods that may foam or shed loose skin during cooking (such as apples or beans), which can block the steam and release valves, but again, check your model. Probably most important is just staying close to the kitchen when pressure cooking so that you can keep an eye on it.

## WHAT COOKS BEST IN A PRESSURE COOKER? ARE THERE FOODS I SHOULD AVOID?

Beans and grains cook up beautifully, and quickly, in the pressure cooker. I tend to cook soups, stews, and vegetables in one-pot meals, but they can be tasty solo, too (though I avoid cooking vegetables alone in an *electric* pressure cooker because they tend to come out overdone). Vegetables don't necessarily cook faster in the pressure cooker, but the flavor can't be beat. Root vegetables in particular, such as potatoes, can cook up in 5 minutes and are always a favorite.

**IS OIL REQUIRED TO PRESSURE COOK?**
There are two points I want to make about using oil. The first is about safety. There was a time when conventional wisdom suggested that all beans must be cooked with oil to avoid foaming and blowing up a pressure cooker. It was about caution, not flavor. With modern-day pressure cookers, there are more safety features to prevent this from happening, but my general word of advice is to use oil—to avoid loose bean skins lodging in the pressure cooker valve—with beans such as fava and soy and even with grains to avoid foaming (more on that in chapter 2). In this book I will be sure to tell you when oil is essential for safety.

My second point about oil is this: fat—such as added oil or vegan butter—does equal flavor, and I use it in many recipes for this purpose. Although this is not a low- or no-fat cookbook, I have made a concerted effort to offer options wherever possible for those of you following a low- or no-oil diet. The option is simply this: Substitute oil with 2 to 4 tablespoons (30 to 60 ml) water or vegetable broth for the sauté portion of a recipe.

**WHAT DOES COOKING AT "HIGH PRESSURE" AND "LOW PRESSURE" MEAN, AND WHEN DO I USE EACH?**
In each recipe you will see the directive "bring to pressure." You do this by turning the stove heat up to a temperature that will bring everything inside to a boil, which usually means medium-high or high heat. Once it has "come to pressure" (i.e., you see or hear a steady stream of steam or gentle rocking motion of the pressure regulator; your manual will tell you what pressure looks or sounds like on your cooker specifically), you reduce the heat to just enough to maintain pressure. In older pressure cooker models this may mean medium-low heat; modern-day pressure cookers can maintain pressure on low and sometimes even on simmer.

I make almost all of my recipes at "high pressure." To do this, simply heat up your covered pressure cooker on high, then once pressure is achieved reduce the heat low enough to maintain pressure.

When cooking at "low pressure"— almost always for quick vegetable dishes— bring to pressure, then simply reduce the heat so that you have a less intense stream of steam or rocking motion of the pressure regulator than at high pressure. Many new models of pressure cookers have an actual high and low setting (often delineated as "1" and "2"). If you see a recipe that states, "bring to pressure," assume high pressure. I only write low when I really want you to cook at low.

**WHAT ARE NATURAL, NORMAL, AND QUICK RELEASE AND HOW DO YOU DO EACH?**
Most pressure cooker recipes will tell you how to release pressure. **Natural pressure release** (or NPR, as it may be called) means that you remove the pres-

sure cooker from the burner and leave it alone. The pressure will come down naturally (refer to your pressure cooker manual for what that may look like, such as the yellow button on the Fagor Splendid or the air vent/cover lock on the Presto handle going down). If pressure doesn't come down naturally in 10 minutes, it's fine to do a quick release (see below).

New-generation pressure cookers, and some electric pressure cookers, have a release valve on the lid, which allows for **normal release**. Just open or press the release valve—don't be alarmed by the steam or sound; that's normal. Pressure will release in a few minutes with the same indications as outlined above. I tend to use normal and quick release for vegetables. For **quick release** hold the covered pressure cooker under cold water (be careful that you don't burn your sink with a hot pressure cooker!) and allow the water to run over the lid (but not the regulator) of the pressure cooker. Pressure will go down in a matter of seconds (longer if you have a whole lot of food in there).

### WHY DO COOKING TIMES VARY?
Pressure cooking is not an exact science. Let me repeat: *It's not an exact science.* Expect some trial and error. I typically err on the side of too much liquid and lower cooking times because I can always bring it back up to pressure and/or simmer to doneness, or drain liquid off. Remember, you can keep cooking *undercooked* food, but overcooked is ovecooked for good.

### WHAT DO I DO IF THE FOOD IS NOT DONE?
As mentioned above, you can always bring it back up to pressure, or simply simmer, uncovered, on the stove until done.

### WILL ELEVATION AFFECT COOKING TIMES?
In a word, yes. The cooking times in this book are based on being at sea level. For my fellow higher-altitude cooks, follow this formula to adjust cook times to your altitude: If you're at 3,000 feet (914 m), immediately add 5 percent more cooking time. For each additional 1,000 feet (305 m), add another 5 percent. I live at 6,000-ish feet (1,829 m) in Colorado, so I add 20 percent more cooking time (5 percent for being at 3,000 feet [914 m] + 15 percent for the additional 3,000 feet [914 m] = 20 percent). I typically opt for the end range of cooking time first and then add my 20 percent—so if black bean cooking time is 18 to 25 minutes, I take the 25 minutes and add 20 percent more time, for 30 minutes total. Grains and veggies, however, tend to cook at the same time as at sea level, so there's no need to adjust time for those.

### WHAT SIZE PRESSURE COOKER SHOULD I BUY?
Most people do just fine with a 6- or 8-quart (5.7 or 7.6 L) pressure cooker. If you typically feed a family of six or more, you may want to consider a 10-quart (9.5 L) or larger pressure cooker.

## WHICH PRESSURE COOKER SHOULD I BUY?

There are three types of pressure cookers used today: first, second, and third generation. First-generation pressure cookers have the "jiggly" pressure regulator on the vent pipe. Second-generation pressure cookers are quieter and have a spring that holds the valve closed until pressure has been achieved. Third-generation pressure cookers are electric. I use all three types and encourage you to choose whichever type fits you best. Cost-wise, pressure cookers generally range from $40 to $200 (£24 to £118). A solid second-generation pressure cooker is about $70 to $80 (£41 to £47). It's a modest investment for a lifetime of quick and easy meals!

## HOW DOES AN ELECTRIC PRESSURE COOKER DIFFER FROM A STOVE TOP PRESSURE COOKER?

Many people opt for an electric pressure cooker because of its modern features (auto start/stop and warming settings) and possibly out of fear of a stove top model. In my experience, electric pressure cookers are excellent for vegetable broth, beans, grains, soups, and stews. The automatic timing feature is terrific—there's nothing like setting up breakfast in the cooker before going to bed and waking up to hot porridge! The downside, in my opinion, is that these devices often require a few extra minutes of cooking. In addition, some electric pressure cookers do not have a sauté function, which means you must either do this separately on the stove top and then add to the pressure cooker, or skip it and miss out on all that rich, added flavor. I should note that there are not separate instructions for electric pressure cookers in this book. If you plan on using one, please refer to your manual for suggested cooking times.

## WHAT DIFFERENCES ARE THERE BETWEEN PRESSURE COOKING ON A GAS OR AN ELECTRIC STOVE?

You have much more control over heat with a gas stove. With an electric stove, it may take more time to reduce pressure. One tactic is to use a second burner at the ideal heat for low pressure and transfer the cooker once pressure is achieved.

## DOES MY PRESSURE COOKER REQUIRE ANY SPECIAL TYPE OF CARE?

Always make sure the rubber gasket is in place and in good shape before using. When it begins to dry out or become stiff it's time for a new one, which you can most likely order from the manufacturer. Also, clean the vents and valves after every use. The owner's manual will explain how to do this. With a little care, your pressure cooker will last you for years and years!

## MORE QUESTIONS?

If there are other questions that come up for you and you can't find the answer throughout this book, ask at the www.veganpressurecooking.com community.

# Cooking Time Charts

Cooking times can vary by the type of pressure cooker, the location (sea level or high elevation), and even the type of stove. Use these general cooking times as a guide, adjusting as necessary to your conditions.

The cook times are the minutes spent at high pressure (or, maintaining pressure). For vegetables, use a quick release; for beans and grains, use a natural release.

## Vegetables

| TYPE OF VEGETABLE | COOK TIME (MINUTES) |
|---|---|
| Asparagus, thick whole | 2 |
| Asparagus, thin whole | 1 to 1 1/2 |
| Beets, large whole | 20 |
| Beets, small whole | 1 to 2 |
| Broccoli, chopped, florets or spears | 2 |
| Brussels sprouts, whole | 4 |
| Carrots, 1/4-inch (6 mm) slices | 1 |
| Carrots, 1-inch (2.5 cm) chunks | 4 |
| Cauliflower, florets | 2 to 3 |
| Corn, kernel | 1 |
| Corn on the cob | 3 |
| Escarole, coarsely chopped | 1 to 2 |
| Kale, coarsely chopped | 1 to 2 |
| Okra, small pods | 2 to 3 |
| Onions, medium whole | 2 to 3 |
| Peas | 1 |
| Potatoes, 1-inch (2.5 cm) cubes | 5 |
| Potatoes, new whole | 5 |
| Potatoes, sweet and yams, 2-inch (5 cm) chunks | 6 to 7 |
| Potatoes, sweet and yams, medium whole | 10 to 11 |
| Spinach, fresh, coarsely chopped | 2 |
| Squash, acorn, halved | 7 |
| Squash, butternut, 1-inch (2.5 cm) chunks | 4 |
| Squash, summer, zucchini, or yellow, 1/2-inch (1.3 cm) slices | 2 |
| Turnips, 1 1/2-inch (3.8 cm) chunks | 3 |
| Turnips, small quartered | 3 |

# Beans

| TYPE OF BEAN | COOK TIME FOR SOAKED BEANS (MINUTES) | COOK TIME FOR UNSOAKED BEANS (MINUTES) |
|---|---|---|
| Adzuki | 5 to 8 | 14 to 20 |
| Black | 7 to 10 | 22 to 24 |
| Black-eyed | 3 to 5 | 6 to 8 |
| Cannellini | 6 to 8 | 25 to 30 |
| Chickpea (garbanzo) | 10 to 15 | 35 to 40 |
| Cranberry | 7 to 10 | 20 to 25 |
| Great Northern | 7 to 10 | 25 to 30 |
| Lentils, brown | n/a | 8 to 10 |
| Lentils, French (green) | n/a | 10 to 12 |
| Lentils, red | n/a | 4 to 6 |
| Lima | 1 to 3 | 4 to 7 |
| Navy (pea) | 5 to 8 | 16 to 20 |
| Pinto | 4 to 6 | 22 to 24 |
| Red kidney | 5 to 8 | 20 to 25 |

# Grains

| TYPE OF GRAIN | LIQUID PER GRAIN (CUPS/ML) | COOK TIME (MINUTES) |
|---|---|---|
| Amaranth | 2/470 ml | 4 to 8 |
| Barley (pearl) | 2/470 ml | 18 to 20 |
| Buckwheat | 2/470 ml | 3 |
| Millet | 2/470 ml | 10 |
| Oats, rolled | 4/940 ml | 6 |
| Oats, steel-cut | 3/705 ml | 5 |
| Polenta, coarse | 4/940 ml | 8 |
| Quinoa | 1½ /352 ml | 1 |
| Rice, basmati | 1½ /352 ml | 4 to 6 |
| Rice, long-grain white | 1½ /352 ml | 4 |
| Rice, wild | 3/705 ml | 22 to 28 |

# Final Tips and Tricks

1. Pressure cookers retain heat really well and get hot, even before being lidded. During the sauté step in a recipe, for instance, you may find some of your vegetables sticking to the bottom of the pan; keep a cup of water or vegetable broth nearby and just add a tablespoon (15 ml) if that happens.

2. Think intuitively! I love mixing and matching beans, greens, and vegetables. Refer to the cooking charts and combine foods with a similar cooking time. You'll have fun!

3. Size matters: Pay attention to the max line on your pressure cooker and make sure you're using a size-appropriate pressure cooker.

4. Don't salt beans while cooking—only once done. (The only exception to this is when you've soaked them overnight and they are part of a larger recipe, such as chili.) I tend to use alternative sodium sources, such as Herbamare, soy sauce, or sea vegetables, and when cooking beans in bulk (for use in other recipes), I don't salt at all. Instead, I stir lemon or lime juice into the beans before storing in the refrigerator or freezer. This allows me the freedom to add a variety of spices, including salt, when using the beans in other dishes.

5. It's okay to have an oops moment. Do you know how many times I've forgotten an ingredient? If you realize you forgot something early on in the process, before coming to pressure, simply quick release (see page 14) as a precaution, open the lid, add what you need, lock the lid in place, and get things going again. If you realize it even later than that, either skip it or quickly cook it separately and add it at the end.

# CHAPTER TWO

# Beans and Grains

Beans, greens, and grains, that's all we vegans eat, right? Hey, like that is a bad thing? True, back in the day when the perception was that only hippies were vegan, the plant-based diet seemed to be filled with brown rice, beans, and spinach. Today veganism is growing and the supermarket aisles prove it.

But let's remember something—beans, greens, and grains are delicious, nutritious, and an important part of the vegan diet. If you want to eat a whole-foods diet, these are your trifecta!

# Bulk Cooking Beans and Grains

Bulk cooking—making food in large batches—expanded the diversity of food in my diet dramatically. Spending just a few hours in the kitchen resulted in food that I could reheat during the week and freeze to use later. Beans and grains are perfect for bulk cooking because they are a staple in a vegan diet and they store well once cooked. I tend to make two grains and two beans each weekend. I freeze half of each and use the other half for meals over three to four days. (Take note: Beans can turn quickly, so eat them up within three days if storing in the refrigerator.) Using this method, I build up a rotation of beans and grains in the freezer and find that each week—through fresh bulk cooking and thawing previously cooked foods—I am eating at least four kinds of beans and four kinds of grains—and with minimal effort!

Recipes with beans and grains can be found in every chapter of this book. Consider this section your go-to when just want to cook up some simple bean and grain staples. Lacking creativity? Opt for a "hippie bowl"—a plate or bowl layered with cooked grains, then beans, topped with cooked or raw veggies, and served with a nut-based sauce.

# Beans Made Simple

Simple fact: I bought my first pressure so that I could make beans in minutes. The mighty legume is a tremendous source of protein in a vegan diet and, frankly, I was tired of buying all of those cans of beans. What keeps most people from making beans from scratch is one thing: time. The pressure cooker removes that obstacle.

Now, to soak or not to soak, that is the question. Many people are drawn to using a pressure cooker to avoid soaking beans (I was), but soaking does have a purpose: It makes beans more digestible and, even in the pressure cooker, they cook more quickly. In my personal experience, they also cook more evenly and, frankly, taste better. If you don't want to soak beans overnight—or you forget to—you can cook unsoaked, dried beans. The cooking time is longer than soaked but still significantly shorter than the conventional stove top method.

When cooking beans you want just the right amount of water. I have seen instructions as diverse as simply covering the beans with water to using 8 cups (2 L) of water. Ultimately, you will find the right ratio for you based on your cooker and your stove, but let's start with the general rule: cover the beans with water, and then add another 1 inch (2.5 cm). More specifically, when I lived at sea level, I used $^1/_2$ cup (120 ml) of liquid to 1 cup (170 g) of soaked (uncooked) beans (or 1:2 ratio) and 2 cups (470 ml) of liquid to 1 cup (200 g) of unsoaked (dried) beans (or 2:1 ratio). That formula worked very well for me there, but now that I live at 6,000 feet (1.8 km), I use a 3:1 ratio of liquid to beans for unsoaked beans. (I use the same ratio as at sea level for soaked beans.) When in doubt, use too much cooking liquid rather than too little. Let me tell you, I've burned some beans and that is no fun: it stinks and it's wasteful.

Finally, avoid salting beans before they are fully cooked. The skin may break and the beans may not cook evenly.

# Italian Lentils

Lentils cook up quickly and are a great staple in the vegan kitchen.
These Italian-flavored lentils are great in a lettuce salad tossed with sundried tomatoes and green olives or added to marinara for a meatier pasta sauce.

||||||||||||||||||||||||||||||||||||||||||||||||||||||||||||||||||||||||||||||||||||||||||||||||||||||||||||||||||||||||||||||||||||||||||||||||||||||||||||||||||||||||||||||||

1 cup (200 g) dried brown lentils, rinsed and drained (no need to soak)

1 cup (235 ml) vegetable broth

1 cup (235 ml) water

$\frac{1}{4}$ teaspoon garlic powder

$\frac{1}{2}$ teaspoon Italian seasoning (or a blend of oregano, basil, marjoram, and parsley)

Add all the ingredients to the pressure cooker. Stir to combine. Cover and bring to pressure. Cook at high pressure for 8 to 10 minutes. Use a quick release.

Yield: 4 servings

# Cinnamon-Curried Chickpeas

I prefer soaking my beans before cooking them in the pressure cooker, but sometimes I want to make a bean on the spur of the moment. This recipe is the best of both worlds because I quick-soak the chickpeas for one hour in baking soda—a culinary trick I learned from television chef Christina Pirello—for a creamier texture. These beans are terrific served over a bed of sautéed greens.

1 cup (200 g) dried chickpeas

1 tablespoon (8 g) baking soda

4 to 5 cups (940 to 1175 ml) water, divided

1 teaspoon extra-virgin olive oil

1 clove garlic, minced

¼ cup (40 g) diced onion

½ teaspoon hot curry powder

¼ teaspoon ground cinnamon

1 bay leaf

½ teaspoon sea salt (optional)

Add the chickpeas, baking soda, and 2 cups (470 ml) of the water to a large bowl and soak for 1 hour. Rinse the chickpeas well and drain.

In an uncovered pressure cooker heat the oil on medium-high heat. Add the garlic and onion and sauté for 3 minutes. Add the curry, cinnamon, and bay leaf and stir well. Stir in the chickpeas and 2 cups (470 ml) of the water.

Cover and bring to pressure. Cook at high pressure for 30 to 35 minutes. Allow for a natural release.

Remove the lid and stir in the sea salt. If the chickpeas are not done, simmer in the uncovered pressure cooker until done, adding more of the remaining 1 cup (235 ml) water, if needed. Remove the bay leaf before serving.

Yield: 4 servings

## Recipe Note

You may use ¼ cup (60 ml) vegetable broth as a substitute for oil.

# Umami Anasazi Beans

**Brightly colored (maroon and white-flecked) anasazi beans are** often used as a replacement for pinto beans (because they contain less gas-producing properties) and are typically found in Mexican dishes made with ham. The secret vegan ingredient in this dish, however, is *umami*, the Japanese word for "pleasant savory taste," which is considered the fifth taste in the culinary world (along with sweet, sour, bitter, and salty). Umami foods and cooking techniques bring a sense of meatiness to vegan dishes and lend a feeling of satiety. The pseudo-caramelized onions, mushrooms, liquid smoke, and miso all add a savory flavor experience—no ham required!

1 cup (200 g) dried anasazi beans, soaked for 12 hours or overnight

1 tablespoon (15 ml) extra-virgin olive oil

2 cups (320 g) half-moon slices onion

½ teaspoon sugar

½ cup (35 g) finely diced mushrooms

¼ teaspoon liquid smoke

1 teaspoon smoked paprika

2 cups (470 ml) vegan beef-style broth

¼ cup (60 ml) water

2 teaspoons red miso

1 teaspoon tamari (optional)

Rinse and drain the soaked beans.

In an uncovered pressure cooker, heat the olive oil on high. Add the onion and sugar and cook on high for 10 minutes. You don't want to burn the onions, but you do want to caramelize them, so stirring frequently is essential, as is adding water (as necessary) to avoid sticking. After 10 minutes, the onions should be soft and brown. Add the beans, mushrooms, liquid smoke, paprika, broth, and water. Stir to combine.

Cover and bring to pressure. Cook at high pressure for 5 to 7 minutes. Allow for a natural release.

Remove the lid and stir in the miso. For a saltier flavor, add the tamari.

Yield: 4 servings

## Recipe Notes

• Serve in a bowl alongside a side of crusty bread to sop up the delicious juice!

• Yellow miso can be substituted but contains less umami.

# Balsamic Black Beans

## Balsamic vinegar is a versatile pantry item. You might be accustomed

to only using it for salads, but it's also lovely for finishing off a pot of beans. The sweet-and-sour flavor makes this a great side dish or as an entrée served over a simply prepared grain, such as quinoa.

1 cup (200 g) dried black beans, soaked for 12 hours or overnight

1 teaspoon extra-virgin olive oil

2 cloves garlic, minced

1 cup (110 g) diced parsnip

$\frac{1}{2}$ teaspoon ground coriander

$\frac{1}{2}$ teaspoon ground cardamom

2 cups (470 ml) water

2 to 3 tablespoons (30 to 45 ml) balsamic vinegar, divided

$\frac{1}{2}$ teaspoon salt (optional)

Rinse and drain the soaked beans.

In an uncovered pressure cooker, heat the oil on medium-high heat. Add the garlic and sauté for a minute or two; you want it soft, but not brown. Add the parsnip, coriander, and cardamom and sauté for 3 to 5 minutes. Add water if needed to keep from sticking. Add the black beans and water. Stir to combine.

Cover and bring to pressure. Cook at high pressure for 4 to 6 minutes. Allow for a natural release.

Remove the lid and stir in 2 tablespoons (30 ml) of the balsamic vinegar. Taste; add the remaining 1 tablespoon (15 ml) vinegar, if desired, and salt to taste.

Yield: 6 servings

## Recipe Notes

• When using vegetables in a basic bean dish (not soup) such as this one, you'll want to opt for soaked beans because their reduced cooking time is more closely matched to the vegetable cooking time; vegetables that cook in 5 to 10 minutes are perfect with a soaked bean that cooks in a similar time.

• Try other root vegetables instead of parsnip, such as carrot, celery, potatoes, beets, or turnips.

• Try using a flavored balsamic vinegar, such as fig, if you like.

# Chili-Style Kidney Beans

Red kidney beans are great in soups and on salads. Once soaked, they cook up in 5 to 8 minutes. Use traditional chili seasoning and you can add these beans to a quick spicy soup, scatter on a taco salad, or stuff in a baked sweet potato and serve with a dollop of vegan sour cream. You can also use pinto beans instead of kidney beans if you prefer.

|||||||||||||||||||||||||||||||||||||||||||||||||||||||||||||||||||||||||||||||||||||||||||||||||||||||||||||||||||||||||||||||||||||

1 cup (200 g) dried red kidney beans, soaked for 12 hours or overnight

1 teaspoon chili powder

1 teaspoon red pepper flakes

1 teaspoon onion powder

½ teaspoon garlic powder

½ teaspoon ground cumin

2 cups (470 ml) water

Rinse and drain the soaked beans. Place all the ingredients in the pressure cooker, cover, bring to pressure, and cook at high pressure for 5 to 8 minutes. Allow for a natural release.

Yield: 6 servings

# Three Bean Delight

This dish, three nutrient-dense beans—pinto, kidney, and adzuki—cooked with a sea vegetable (kombu) and served over brown rice, is a nod to the macrobiotic philosophy that health, longevity, and healing can be obtained through a simple, plant-based diet. Serve as an entrée, surrounded by steamed vegetables and a simple grain side dish.

1 teaspoon extra-virgin olive oil

½ cup (80 g) diced Vidalia or other sweet onion

2 cloves garlic, minced

2 cups (400 g) mixed dried pinto, red kidney, and adzuki beans

1-inch (2.5 cm) strip kombu

4 to 5 cups (940 to 1175 ml) water

½ to 1 teaspoon dulse flakes

In an uncovered pressure cooker, heat the oil on medium heat. Add the onion and garlic and sauté for 3 minutes, or until the onions are translucent. Stir in the beans, kombu, and water.

Cover and bring to pressure. Cook at high pressure for 22 to 25 minutes. Allow for a natural release.

Remove the lid and taste for doneness. If the beans need to be cooked a bit longer, simmer until done. Stir in the dulse flakes.

Yield: 4 to 6 servings

## Recipe Notes

• If you want to leave out the oil, substitute ¼ cup (60 ml) water or vegetable broth.

• Kombu and dulse flakes are sea vegetables, often referred to as seaweed. These vegetables, which also include nori, arame, and kelp, play a big role in Japanese cooking. They are usually sold dried and can be added to soups or used to make vegetarian sushi. All add a deep umami flavor to dishes.

• Herbamare, an herb seasoning blended with natural salt, or other natural salt alternatives can be substituted for the sea vegetables.

# Grains Made Simple

Grains are often a staple in a vegan diet—they are in mine—because they are high in fiber and contain protein, B vitamins, and zinc. By simply adding grains such as brown rice, oats, and barley, you will boost the nutrient density of any meal and it brings such a great diversity of taste and texture to meals.

In addition to serving as a side dish or as a base to a "hippie bowl" layered with grain, beans, and vegetables, they are excellent in soups and stews and make for a terrific breakfast.

Note that some grains, such as oats, may foam, so be sure to pay attention to the maximum fill line and the precautions outlined by your particular pressure cooker.

# Dill Long-Grain White Rice

Dill brings big taste to the simplest of dishes. Quickly sauté green beans in garlic and serve over this rice, topped with almond slivers, for a flavor-packed meal.

|||||||||||||||||||||||||||||||||||||||||||||||||||||||||||||||||||||||||||||||||||||||||||||||||||||||||

1 teaspoon extra-virgin olive oil

3 cloves garlic, minced

1 teaspoon dried dill, plus more for garnish

1 cup (190 g) long-grain white rice

1 1/2 cups (355 ml) water

1 tablespoon (15 ml) lemon juice

1/2 to 1 teaspoon salt

In an uncovered pressure cooker, heat the oil on medium heat. Add the garlic and sauté for 2 minutes, or until softened. Add the dill, rice, and water. Stir to combine.

Cover and bring to pressure. Cook at high pressure for 18 to 25 minutes. Allow for a natural release.

Stir in the lemon juice, add salt to taste, and garnish with extra dill.

Yield: 4 servings

# Brown Rice

Brown rice is an essential in my house. I love having it on hand, and in the freezer, because it's great in soups, in a hippie bowl (see page 20), as a simple side, or mixed with beans.

|||||||||||||||||||||||||||||||||||||||||||||||||||||||||||||||||||||||||||||||||||||||||||||||||||||||||

1 cup (190 g) brown rice

1 1/2 cups (355 ml) water or vegetable broth

Place the rice and water in the pressure cooker. Cover and bring to pressure. Cook at high pressure for 18 to 25 minutes. Allow for a natural release.

Yield: 4 servings

# Mushroom Rice

## Serve this mushroom rice with a lightly seasoned Asian stir-fry or

roll it up in a nori sheet with your favorite vegetables for a hearty vegan sushi roll. When selecting mushrooms, shiitake, cremini, or maitake are all nutrient-packed, flavorful choices.

1 teaspoon sesame oil

1 cup (70 g) chopped or sliced mushrooms

1 cup (190 g) long-grain brown rice

1 ½ cups (355 ml) vegetable broth

1 to 2 tablespoons (15 to 30 ml) tamari

In an uncovered pressure cooker, heat the oil on medium heat. Add the mushrooms and sauté for 3 minutes. Add the rice and broth. Stir to combine.

Cover and bring to pressure. Cook at high pressure for 22 minutes. Allow for a natural release.

Remove the lid and stir in the tamari to taste.

Yield: 4 servings

# Mint Basil Brown Rice

I love this rice with a simple, steamed vegetable. It's also terrific cold, tossed in a salad.

||||||||||||||||||||||||||||||||||||||||||||||||||||

2 cloves garlic, minced

1/4 cup (24 g) chopped fresh mint, plus more for garnish

1 tablespoon (2 g) chopped dried chives or 1/3 cup (15 g) chopped fresh

1 cup (190 g) short- or long-grain brown rice

1 1/2 cups (355 ml) water or no- or low-sodium vegetable broth

1/2 to 1 teaspoon sea salt

Place the garlic, mint, chives, rice, and water in the pressure cooker. Stir to combine. Cover and bring to pressure. Cook at high pressure for 22 minutes. Allow for a natural release. Add salt to taste. Serve garnished with mint.

Yield: 4 servings

# Spanish Rice

Spanish rice is a great side when serving a traditional Mexican meal, but I particularly love it as filling for a taco or in a taco salad.

||||||||||||||||||||||||||||||||||||||||||||||||||||||||

1 tablespoon (15 ml) olive oil

2 cloves garlic, minced

1/2 cup (80 g) finely chopped onion

2 cups (380 g) short-grain brown rice

3 cups (705 ml) vegetable broth

1 tablespoon (16 g) tomato paste

1/2 cup (90 g) diced tomato

1/2 teaspoon cumin

1/2 teaspoon paprika

1/4 to 1/2 teaspoon salt

1 teaspoon chili powder (more if you like heat!)

In an uncovered pressure cooker, heat the oil on medium-high. Add the garlic and onion and sauté for 3 minutes, or until the onions are translucent. Add the rice and sauté for about 5 minutes, until the rice browns slightly. Add the broth, tomato paste, diced tomato, and seasonings. Stir to combine.

Cover and bring to pressure. Cook at high pressure for 20 to 22 minutes. Allow for a natural release.

Yield: 8 servings

# Freekeh

Freekeh, or young green wheat, is a popular grain in Middle Eastern
cooking and has a lovely nutty flavor and chewy texture. Rich in protein, vitamins, and minerals,
serve it with curried beans or dal and a leafy green for a complete meal.

||||||||||||||||||||||||||||||||||||||||||||||||||||||||||||||||||||||||||||||||||||||||||||||||||||||||

**1 cup (160 g) freekeh**

**2 ½ cups (588 ml) water**

Combine the freekeh and water in the pressure cooker.
Cover and bring to pressure. Cook at high pressure for
6 minutes. Allow for a natural release; if after 10 minutes
the pressure has still not come down fully, manually
release.

Yield: 4 to 6 servings

# Basic Quinoa

Quinoa cooks up in one minute in the pressure cooker. You read
that right! One minute at pressure and then allow for a natural release (up to ten minutes).
Make this hearty grain staple—which is actually a seed (and an honorary legume)—and use it in
endless dishes.

|||||||||||||||||||||||||||||||||||||||||||||||||||||||||||||||||||||||||||||||||||||||||||||||||||||||||||||||||||||||||||||||

1 cup (175 g) quinoa

1 ½ cups (355 ml) water or broth

½ teaspoon sea salt (optional)

Rinse and drain the quinoa. Place all the ingredients in
the pressure cooker. Stir to combine.

Cover and bring to pressure. Cook at high pressure for
1 minute. Allow for a natural release; if after 10 minutes
the pressure has still not come down fully, manually
release. Fluff and serve.

Yield: 4 servings

## Recipe Note

My favorite ways to eat quinoa include:

• Tossed in a salad

• As a warm breakfast cereal, drizzled with maple
syrup and topped with chopped pecans

• As the base to vegetable or bean soup

• In a "hippie bowl" (see page 20).

# Quinoa Pilaf

You can use this basic recipe and mix and match flavors for a variety of pilaf dishes. Simply substitute the parsley and thyme for other flavor profiles. For example, ginger and paprika with curry vegetable broth and chopped cashews make for a tasty Indian-style pilaf.

||||||||||||||||||||||||||||||||||||||||||||||||||||||||||||||||||||||||||||||||||||||||||

1 cup (175 g) quinoa

1 teaspoon walnut oil

$\frac{1}{2}$ cup (80 g) chopped red onion

1 cup (130 g) diced carrot

$1\frac{1}{2}$ cups (355 ml) vegetable broth

$\frac{1}{2}$ teaspoon dried parsley

$\frac{1}{2}$ teaspoon dried thyme

$\frac{1}{2}$ teaspoon sea salt

$\frac{1}{4}$ to $\frac{1}{2}$ cup (30 to 60 g) chopped walnuts

Chopped fresh parsley or thyme, for garnish

Rinse and drain the quinoa.

In an uncovered pressure cooker, heat the oil on medium heat. Add the onion and carrot and sauté for 3 minutes. Add the vegetable broth, dried parsley, dried thyme, salt, and quinoa. Stir to combine.

Cover and bring to pressure. Cook at high pressure for 1 minute. Allow for a natural release; if after 10 minutes the pressure has still not come down fully, manually release.

Fluff the quinoa before gently mixing in the walnuts. Serve with a garnish of fresh parsley or thyme.

Yield: 4 servings

## Recipe Note

If you don't have walnut oil, substitute vegetable oil or $\frac{1}{4}$ cup (60 ml) vegetable broth or water.

# Italian Pearl Barley

## Popular in hearty soups and

stews, pearl barley is also used in orzotto, which is similar to risotto. With just a few seasonings, this is a terrific side to Mediterranean main dishes.

||||||||||||||||||||||||||||||||||||||||||||||||||||||||

**1 cup (200 g) pearl barley**

**3 cups (705 ml) vegetable broth**

**1/2 teaspoon dried oregano**

**1/2 teaspoon dried basil**

Add all the ingredients to the pressure cooker. Cover and bring to pressure. Cook at high pressure for 18 to 20 minutes. Use a quick release.

Yield: 4 to 6 servings

# Basic Pearl Barley

## This adaptable grain can be

used in place of brown rice, as an alternative to oatmeal for breakfast, as a hearty addition to a soup or stew, and even in risotto. I add it to Italian-style hippie bowls such as the Mediterranean Beans with Greens on page 144.

||||||||||||||||||||||||||||||||||||||||||||||||||||||||

**1 cup (200 g) pearl barley**

**2 cups (470 ml) water**

Add the barley and water to the pressure cooker. Cover and bring to pressure. Cook at high pressure for 18 to 20 minutes. Allow for a natural release.

Yield: 4 servings

# Bulgur Paprika

**Bulgur wheat is a chewy grain** that bulks up soups, stews, and salads. It's also a great replacement for rice. The addition of garlic and paprika (I prefer smoked or Hungarian in this dish) brings an exotic aroma and vibrant color to a very simple side dish—excellent alongside chickpeas or black beans.

‖‖‖‖‖‖‖‖‖‖‖‖‖‖‖‖‖‖‖‖‖‖‖‖‖‖‖‖‖‖‖‖‖‖‖

1 teaspoon extra-virgin olive oil

3 cloves garlic, minced

1 tablespoon (7 g) paprika

1 cup (185 g) bulgur

1 teaspoon sea salt

1³/₄ cups (411 ml) water

In an uncovered pressure cooker, heat the olive oil on medium heat. Add the garlic and sauté for no more than 30 seconds. Add the paprika, bulgur, salt, and water. Stir to combine.

Cover and bring to pressure. Cook at high pressure for 5 minutes. Allow for a natural release; if after 10 minutes the pressure has still not come down fully, manually release. Fluff the bulgur gently with a fork.

Yield: 4 to 6 servings

# Wild Rice with Dried Cherries and Cranberries ▶

**Just right for the holiday table,** this is a great side with a vegan roast—or add cooked lentils and let it stand alone as a festive entrée. If you want to skip the oil, add ¹/₄ cup (60 ml) water or vegetable broth.

‖‖‖‖‖‖‖‖‖‖‖‖‖‖‖‖‖‖‖‖‖‖‖‖‖‖‖‖‖‖‖‖‖‖‖

1 teaspoon extra-virgin olive oil

¹/₄ cup (25 g) chopped celery

¹/₄ cup (40 g) diced onion

1 cup (160 g) wild rice

1 cup (120 g) mix of dried cranberries and dried cherries

¹/₂ teaspoon dried thyme

¹/₂ teaspoon dried sage

3 to 3¹/₂ cups (705 to 825 ml) water

Salt, to taste

In an uncovered pressure cooker, heat the oil on medium-high. Add the celery and onion and sauté until the celery is soft, 3 to 4 minutes. Add the rice, dried fruit, thyme, sage, and water. Stir to combine.

Cover and bring to pressure. Cook at high pressure for 22 to 25 minutes. Allow for a natural release. Add salt to taste.

Yield: 4 servings

# Hot Breakfasts
# Made Simple

Porridge and hot cereals are my favorite breakfast and a great way to fit more whole grains into your diet. I tend to mix and match grains with similar cooking times and then use a variety of liquids. Water is always an option but sometimes mixing things up with a plant milk, or even a vegetable broth, adds a special creaminess and intensified flavor profile.

   If you're using an electric pressure cooker you can easily set up your unit to automatically begin cooking before you wake up—there's nothing better than waking up to a hot breakfast!

# Couscous, Oatmeal, and Veggie Porridge

I love a savory breakfast, and adding vegetables to a traditional oat or porridge dish can do just the trick. For a richer flavor consider using a vegan-beef or chicken-style broth. Toasted nuts or seeds—consider tamari seasoned pumpkin seeds—make for a great garnish, too.

2 tablespoons (28 g) vegan butter

¼ cup (40 g) diced yellow onion

2 cups (260 g) finely, evenly diced carrots

5 cups (1.2 L ml) water

1 cup (175 g) couscous

1 cup (80 g) rolled oats

1 teaspoon sea salt

½ teaspoon cinnamon

In an uncovered pressure cooker heat the vegan butter on medium-high heat. Add the onion and sauté for 1 minute. Add the carrots, and then add the water, couscous, oats, salt, and cinnamon. Stir to combine.

Cover and bring to pressure. Cook at high pressure for 5 minutes. Allow for a natural release; if after 10 minutes the pressure has still not come down fully, manually release. Remove the lid, fluff, and serve.

Yield: 4 servings

## Recipe Note

For added creaminess, substitute coconut or almond milk for the water.

# Brown Rice and Farro Porridge

Farro has twice the fiber and protein of traditional wheat, making this a healthy breakfast alternative. Farro has a natural, nutty undertone with a hint of cinnamon, making it an ideal addition to a savory breakfast dish.

|||||||||||||||||||||||||||||||||||||||||||||||||||||||||||||||||||||||||||||||||||||||||||||||||||||||||||||||||||||||||||||||||||||||||

½ cup (95 g) short-grain brown rice, rinsed and drained

½ cup (90 g) farro, rinsed and drained

½ cup (65 g) frozen corn

2 ¼ cups (530 ml) water

Pinch of salt

Fresh basil, for garnish (optional)

Add the rice, farro, corn, water, and salt to the pressure cooker. Stir to combine.

Cover and bring to pressure. Cook at high pressure for 20 minutes. Allow for a natural release; if after 10 minutes the pressure has still not come down fully, manually release. Garnish with basil.

Yield: 4 to 6 servings

# Apple Pie Steel-Cut Oats

Dessert for breakfast? When it's this nutritious, why not? Well, this isn't exactly dessert, but it is an especially sweet, hot breakfast. Peaches and berries are a great substitute for the apple, as are raisins or dried cranberries for the dates.

1 cup (80 g) steel-cut oats

1 cup (235 ml) almond milk

2 cups (470 ml) water

1 cup (150 g) diced apple

1 large medjool date, chopped

½ teaspoon ground cinnamon

Pinch of sea salt

Add all the ingredients to the pressure cooker. Cover and bring to pressure. Cook at pressure for 3 minutes. Allow for a natural release.

Yield: 4 servings

## Recipe Note

Play with the liquid, just keep the ratio intact! Replacing some of the water with almond, soy, or coconut milk makes for a creamy texture.

# Savory Oat Porridge

## Pumpkin seeds, almonds, and

vegetable broth turn breakfast on its ear with another savory oat option.

|||||||||||||||||||||||||||||||||||||||||||||||||

1 cup (80 g) rolled oats (not instant)

¼ cup (20 g) steel-cut oats

1 tablespoon (8 g) amaranth

¼ cup (30 g) pepitas (pumpkin seeds), plus more for garnish

¼ cup (27 g) almond slivers

2 tablespoons (14 g) nutritional yeast flakes

1¼ cups (295 ml) low-sodium vegetable broth

1 ¼ cups (295 ml) unflavored flaxseed milk (or other plant-based milk)

Herbamare or sea salt, to taste

Add the rolled oats, steel-cut oats, amaranth, pepitas, almonds, nutritional yeast, broth, and milk to the pressure cooker. Stir to combine.

Cover and bring to pressure and cook at high pressure for 3 minutes. Allow for a normal release.

Add Herbamare to taste and garnish with additional pepitas.

Yield: 4 to 6 servings

# Pumpkin Spice Porridge

## The first time I made this hot

breakfast bowl was on a cold Colorado morning, a few days before Thanksgiving. It's now a holiday favorite. If you can't find pumpkin spice coconut milk at the store (it is a seasonal product), just substitute 2 cups (470 ml) regular coconut milk plus 1 tablespoon (6 g) pumpkin pie spice.

|||||||||||||||||||||||||||||||||||||||||||||||||||||

½ cup (88 g) quinoa

¼ cup (32 g) amaranth

¼ cup (44 g) couscous

2 cups (470 ml) pumpkin spice coconut milk, such as So Delicious

¼ cup (60 ml) water

Pumpkin seeds, for garnish

Dried cranberries, for garnish

Add the quinoa, amaranth, couscous, coconut milk, and water to the pressure cooker. Stir to combine.

Cover and bring to pressure. Cook at high pressure for 10 minutes. Allow for a natural release.

Garnish with the pumpkin seeds and dried cranberries.

Yield: 4 to 6 servings

# Multigrain and TVP Hot Cereal

TVP, or textured vegetable protein, is a soy-based product that boosts the nutrition level of this cereal and will keep you satisfied all morning. For a savory cereal, use vegetable broth instead of water and serve with a salty nut; for a sweeter version, use almond or coconut milk instead of water and top with dried fruit.

|||||||||||||||||||||||||||||||||||||||||||||||||||||||||||||||||||||||||||||||||||||||||||||||||||||||||||||||||||||||||||

**1 cup (100 g) multigrain cereal mix**

**½ cup (50 g) TVP**

**3 cups (705 ml) water**

Add all the ingredients to the pressure cooker. Stir to combine. Cover and bring to pressure. Cook at high pressure for 4 minutes. Allow for a natural release.

Yield: 2 to 3 servings

# Oat, Amaranth, and Carrot Porridge

## Similar to the couscous porridge on page 45, this recipe has a

decreased cooking time. Consider replacing the carrots with 1 cup (150 g) of vegetables that cook up in about four minutes: cubed butternut squash, cauliflower florets, or cubed fingerling potatoes.

|||||||||||||||||||||||||||||||||||||||||||||||||||||||||||||||||||||||||||||||||||||||||||||||||||||||||||||||||||||

2 tablespoons (28 g) vegan butter

¼ cup (40 g) diced yellow onion

2 carrots, diced

1 cup (80 g) rolled oats

1 cup (130 g) amaranth

2½ cups (588 ml) water

1 teaspoon salt

½ teaspoon ground cinnamon

In an uncovered pressure cooker, heat the vegan butter on medium heat. Add the onion and carrots and sauté until the onions are translucent, 3 to 4 minutes. Add the oats, amaranth, water, salt, and cinnamon. Stir to combine.

Cover and bring to pressure. Cook at high pressure for 4 minutes. Allow for a natural release.

Yield: 4 servings

# CHAPTER THREE

# Soups and Stews

I bought my first pressure cooker to make quick-cooking beans and grains. I fell in love with my pressure cooker when I realized I could also make soups and stews in no time at all—often featuring those beans and grains! Of course, most soups can be made with water, but I find using vegetable broth is a great way to add flavor. If in chapter 2 I convinced you to quit buying canned beans, perhaps the first thing I can do in this chapter is encourage you to start making your own vegetable broth—it's so darn easy! Throughout this book whenever I call for vegetable broth, consider using your very own homemade broth.

# Basic Vegetable Broth

**Years ago, while interviewing a chef in New York for a piece I was** writing for *The Journal News*, he shared this tip with me: Adding fruit—such as peaches, pears, or apples—to vegetable broths brings flavor and also keeps the broth clear. This works particularly well for making broth for "light" or cream soups. My recipe is inspired by that tip!

1 peach, quartered

2 apples, quartered

1 medium onion, quartered

4 cloves garlic, chopped
(peel and all)

8 carrots, halved

6 stalks celery, halved

1 tomato, quartered

6 whole romaine lettuce leaves

1 teaspoon avocado oil
(optional)

8 cups (2 L) water

½ teaspoon dried oregano

½ teaspoon dried sage

½ teaspoon dried sweet basil

½teaspoon dried whole
(rubbed) rosemary

1 teaspoon sea salt (optional)

Place all the ingredients in the pressure cooker. Stir to combine.

Cover and bring to pressure. Cook at high pressure for 15 to 30 minutes (for a richer broth, opt for 30 minutes).

Remove from the heat and allow for a natural release. Remove the lid from the pressure cooker.

Strain the broth through a fine-mesh strainer or cheesecloth. Use immediately or store in an airtight glass jar or container for up to 1 week; freeze in a heavy-duty freezer bag for 3 to 6 months.

Yield: 6 to 8 cups (1.4 to 2 L)

# Vegetable Scrap Broth

While not the most appealing recipe title, this is my go-to method
for making delicious, homemade vegetable broth on a weekly basis. I save vegetable and fruit
scraps throughout the week and store them in the freezer in a sturdy plastic bag. This reduces
waste and it makes a practical, flavorful vegetable broth to use when cooking soups, grains, and
beans, and for reheating bulk-cooked foods.

1 gallon (3.8 L) freezer bag full
   of vegetable scraps

8 cups (2 L) water

2 bay leaves

½ teaspoon each of 3 or
   4 spices of choice

1 teaspoon sea salt (optional)

Thaw (or partially thaw) the frozen vegetable scraps. Rinse well and drain.

Place the vegetables in the pressure cooker and add the water and seasonings. Stir to combine.

Cover and bring to pressure. Cook at high pressure 15 to 30 minutes (for a richer broth, opt for 30 minutes). Allow for a natural release.

Remove the lid from the pressure cooker. Strain the broth through a fine-mesh strainer or cheesecloth.

If not using immediately, store in an airtight glass jar or container for 3 to 5 days, or freeze in a heavy-duty freezer bag for 3 to 6 months.

Yield: 8 cups (2 L)

## Recipe Notes

• Some of my favorite scraps include red and yellow onion pieces, including peel; garlic and skin; asparagus stems; tomatoes; lettuce, such as romaine, endive, and radicchio; carrot and celery ends; bell or sweet pepper ends and seeds; mushroom stems; spinach; and zucchini. Avoid starchy vegetables such as potatoes or vegetables from the cabbage family—including all types of cabbage, kale, and even Brussels sprouts—as they can become bitter.

• For a classic spice combo, use ½ teaspoon each rosemary, thyme, basil, and oregano.

# Easy Black Bean Soup

## I started making an easy

black bean soup on the stove top: canned beans, salsa, and veggie broth. This is an equally simple version for the pressure cooker.

||||||||||||||||||||||||||||||||||||||||||||||||||

1 cup (200 g) dried black beans, soaked for 12 hours or overnight

1 teaspoon extra-virgin olive oil or 1/4 cup (60 ml) water or vegetable broth

1 carrot, diced

1 stalk celery, chopped

1/2 cup (80 g) diced onion

2 cloves garlic, minced

4 cups (940 ml) vegetable broth

1 cup (235 ml) water

1 cup (260 g) fresh salsa

Rinse the beans and drain well.

In an uncovered pressure cooker, heat the oil on medium-high. Add the carrot, celery, onion, and garlic and sauté for 1 minute. Add the beans, broth, water, and salsa. Stir to combine.

Cover and bring to pressure. Cook at high pressure for 4 to 6 minutes. Allow for a natural release.

Yield: 4 to 6 servings

# Garam Masala Lentil Soup

## Garam masala and cinnamon

fill this simple recipe with flavor.

||||||||||||||||||||||||||||||||||||||||||||||||||

1 3/4 cups (350 g) dried brown or green lentils

1 tablespoon (15 ml) vegetable oil

2 tablespoons (20 g) finely diced shallot

1 cup (130 g) diced carrots

1 cup (120 g) diced celery

1/2 teaspoon garam masala

1/2 teaspoon ground cinnamon

1/2 teaspoon cumin

1 bay leaf

2 cups (470 ml) vegetable broth

3 cups (705 ml) water

1/4 to 1/2 teaspoon sea salt (optional)

**Freshly ground black pepper**

Rinse and drain the lentils.

In an uncovered pressure cooker, heat the oil on medium heat. Add the shallot, carrots, and celery and sauté for 3 to 5 minutes, until the shallot and celery are soft. Add the garam masala, cinnamon, cumin, bay leaf, and lentils and stir well. Add the vegetable broth and water and stir to combine.

Cover and bring to pressure. Cook at high pressure for 7 to 10 minutes. Allow for a natural release.

Remove the cover and stir in the salt to taste. Remove the bay leaf before serving. Serve with freshly ground black pepper.

Yield: 6 servings

# White Beans and Greens Soup

Packed with leafy greens and beans, this soup is a nutrient-dense meal. It's lightly seasoned so that you can play with flavors you love by stirring them in after tasting. During a recent cooking class my students opted for balsamic vinegar and ground black pepper to bring out the sweet and spicy in the soup, and it was terrific. For something zestier, add chili powder or chipotle powder while cooking and stir in hot sauce before serving. I serve this soup over cooked quinoa to make this a filling dinner entrée.

1½ cups (300 g) dried cannellini beans, soaked for 12 hours or overnight

1 tablespoon (15 ml) vegetable oil (optional)

4 large cloves garlic, minced

2 cups (320 g) diced carrots

1 cup (160 g) diced onion

1 cup (120 g) diced celery

2 cups (140 g) sliced cremini, shiitake, maitake, or baby bella mushrooms

1 bay leaf

2 tablespoons (3 g) dried herbes de Provence

½ teaspoon freshly ground black pepper, plus more for serving

1 teaspoon red pepper flakes

5 cups (1.2 L ml) vegetable broth

2 cups (470 ml) water

¼ cup (64 g) tomato paste

8 cups (400 g) loosely packed greens

Juice of 1 large lemon (about 3 tablespoons, or 45 ml)

1 to 1½ teaspoons salt (optional)

Rinse and the drain beans.

In an uncovered pressure cooker, heat the oil on medium-high. Add the garlic, carrots, onion, and celery and sauté for 3 minutes. Add the mushrooms and seasonings and sauté for another 3 to 5 minutes. Add the vegetable broth, water, and tomato paste. Mix well. Add the beans and greens. Stir to combine.

Cover and bring to pressure. Cook at high pressure for 6 to 8 minutes. Allow for a natural release.

Remove the lid, stir in the lemon juice and taste before adding salt. Remove the bay leaf before serving. Serve with freshly ground black pepper

Yield: 6 servings

## Recipe Note

Baby spinach, kale, bok choy, arugula, collard greens, and Swiss chard are all excellent greens in this soup; try a combo of three or four.

# Curried Mung Bean Stew

The mung bean is often used in Asian cuisine. This quick-cooking legume is super-nutritious—packed with protein, dietary fiber, potassium, iron, and magnesium—and is fantastic in Indian-style fare. Curry bullion cubes are great for this, or mix 2 cups (470 ml) water with 2 teaspoons curry powder.

1 teaspoon vegetable oil

2 cloves garlic, minced

1 cup (160 g) diced onion

½ cup (65 g) chopped carrot

1 cup (110 g) cubed sweet potatoes

½ cup (60 g) chopped celery

3 cups (150 g) loosely packed collard green strips

1 teaspoon ground ginger or 1 tablespoon (6 g) minced fresh

¼ teaspoon turmeric

¼ teaspoon paprika

2 cups (470 ml) curry broth

1 cup (235 ml) water

1 cup (200 g) dried mung beans

2 tablespoons (45 ml) lemon juice

½ teaspoon sea salt

In an uncovered pressure cooker, heat the oil on medium heat, add the garlic, onion, carrot, potatoes, and celery and sauté for 5 minutes. Add the collard greens, ginger, turmeric, paprika, curry broth, water, and mung beans. Stir to combine.

Cover and bring to pressure. Cook at high pressure for 6 to 8 minutes. Allow for a natural release.

Stir in the lemon juice and add salt to taste.

Yield: 4 servings

# Potato Soup

One of my all-time cherished food memories is my dad making a very simple potato soup: boiled potatoes, onions, and celery cooked in whole milk and butter. I love making familiar foods vegan, and this may be one of my favorites. Healthier and cooked in less than half the time, it warms my heart and belly just the same as the original.

2 to 3 tablespoons (28 to 42 g) vegan butter

3 cloves garlic, minced

1 package (14 ounces, or 392 g) soft tofu

1 cup (235 ml) almond milk

2 tablespoons (30 ml) lemon juice

1/2 teaspoon salt

1 teaspoon dried dill

4 cups (440 g) diced potatoes

2 cups (140 g) sliced mushrooms

2 cups (320 g) sliced onion, cut into half-moons

1 cup (130 g) chopped carrot

1 cup (120 g) chopped celery

4 cups (940 ml) vegetable broth

Ground black pepper, to taste

In an uncovered pressure cooker, heat the butter on medium-high heat. Add the garlic and sauté for a minute.

In a blender or food processor, pulse the tofu, almond milk, lemon juice, salt, and dill until creamy.

Add the potatoes, mushrooms, onion, carrots, and celery to the pressure cooker, mixing well. Pour the tofu mixture into the pressure cooker. Stir in the vegetable broth. (Tip: As a way to get the remaining tofu cream out of the blender, first pour the vegetable broth into the blender and pulse quickly; then pour into the pot.)

Cover and bring to pressure. Cook at high pressure for 5 minutes. Use a quick release. Serve with freshly ground black pepper.

Yield: 8 servings

## Recipe Notes

• No need to press or drain the tofu in this recipe. Though harder to find at standard grocery stores, boxed silken tofu—typically found in the Asian foods aisle—works very well in this soup.

• Yam, sweet, or russet potatoes are terrific in this recipe; try using a combination of all three.

# Creamy Kale Miso Soup

I created this soup for my book *Vegan for Her* and it became my
go-to cooking demonstration recipe at vegetarian food festivals and grocery stores. Why? It's simple and it's packed with nutrients. Don't worry about details when it comes to chopping and dicing because the soup will get transferred to the blender and those blades will do all the work.

1 to 2 teaspoons vegetable oil

4 cloves garlic, cut in half

1 small sweet onion, quartered

2 medium carrots, cut into
  2- to 3-inch (5 to 7.5 cm)
  pieces

4 cups (940 ml) low-sodium
  vegetable broth

1 package (12 ounces, or 344 g)
  package silken (light
  firm) tofu

1 bunch kale (about 6 ounces
  [168 g] off the stem), plus a
  few leaves for garnish

¼ cup (63 g) yellow miso

Ground black pepper, to taste

In an uncovered pressure cooker, heat the oil on medium-high. Add the garlic, onion, and carrots and sauté for 5 minutes (add liquid if it begins to stick). The onion pieces will begin to brown; this is a semicaramelizing step that brings out so much flavor. Stir frequently.

Add the vegetable broth and tofu. Crumble the tofu into pieces with a spoon. Add the kale and stir to combine.

Cover and bring to pressure. Cook at high pressure for 4 minutes. Allow for a natural release; if after 10 minutes the pressure has still not come down fully, manually release. Remove the lid and stir in the miso.

Transfer to a blender (no more than 3 cups [705 ml] of hot soup at a time) and blend for 20 to 30 seconds, until the kale leaves are completely blended. Note: Hot soup expands in the blender, so pay heed to using only 3 cups (705 ml) of soup at a time and place a hand towel over the top of the blender for an added measure of safety.

Serve with black pepper and garnish with extra kale.

Yield: 6 servings

## Recipe Note

Because we're using miso in this recipe, low-sodium broth is very important—even better, use some of your own, no-sodium homemade broth.

# Chik'n Lentil Noodle Soup

**This soup is a reader favorite on my blog, I suspect because it is** reminiscent of a childhood favorite for many of us—and because it's incredibly easy to prepare and delicious! The "chicken" flavoring is simply seasoning. I use Butler Chik-Style seasoning, though your favorite brand of dry seasoning will do just fine. This is rich in protein and packed with healthy vegetables.

1 teaspoon extra-virgin olive oil

3 cloves garlic, finely diced

1 large onion, diced

2 cups (200 g) green beans (fresh or frozen), snapped into bite-size pieces

1 cup (130 g) chopped carrots

1 cup (120 g) chopped celery

2 teaspoons vegan chicken-flavored seasoning

1 bay leaf

½ teaspoon dried sage

1 cup (200 g) dried brown lentils, rinsed and drained

4 ounces (112 g) soba noodles

4 cups (940 ml) vegetable broth

1 to 1½ cups (235 to 355 ml) water

In an uncovered pressure cooker, heat the oil on medium-high. Add the garlic, onions, green beans, carrots, and celery and sauté for about 3 minutes. Add the chicken-flavored seasoning, bay leaf, and sage and sauté for another 2 minutes. Add the lentils, noodles, vegetable both, and water. Stir to combine.

Cover and to bring to pressure. Cook at high pressure for 8 minutes. Use a quick release.

Sample both the lentils and the noodles. If they are not cooked through, simmer on low in the uncovered pressure cooker until done, adding more water if necessary. Remove the bay leaf before serving.

Yield: 4 to 6 servings

## Recipe Notes

• You can find vegan chicken-style seasoning or bouillon cubes at most grocery stores.

• To deepen the flavor further, use vegan chicken broth instead of vegetable broth.

# Portobello Mushroom and Barley Soup

The first time I made this recipe I felt like a culinary rock star: a homemade soup made with whole vegetables, whole grains, and my homemade vegetable stock made completely from more whole vegetables. Quick to prepare and quick to the table, this substantial soup stands alone as a lunch or dinner entrée.

1 teaspoon vegetable oil

2 cloves garlic, minced

½ cup (80 g) diced onion

3 stalks celery, chopped

2 carrots, diced

2 large portobello mushrooms (6 ounces [168 g]), sliced lengthwise, then sliced again

1 tomato, diced

¾ cup (200 g) pearl barley, rinsed and drained

3 cups (705 ml) vegetable broth

4 cups (940 ml) water

2 sprigs fresh thyme or 1 teaspoon dried

½ to 1 teaspoon salt

Ground black pepper

In an uncovered pressure cooker, heat the oil on medium-high. Add garlic and onion and sauté for 2 to 3 minutes, until the onion is soft. Add the celery and carrot and sauté for another 3 to 5 minutes, until the celery is soft. Add the mushrooms, tomato, barley, broth, water, and thyme. Stir to combine.

Cover and bring to pressure. Cook at high pressure for 20 minutes. Allow for a natural release.

Remove the cover and stir in the salt. Serve with freshly ground black pepper.

Yield: 6 to 8 servings

## Recipe Note

You may use ¼ cup (60 ml) vegetable broth as a substitute for oil.

# Very Veggie Split Pea Soup

The "very" in this recipe refers to the fresh green juice. If you don't have a juicer, consider picking up 32 ounces (1 L) of your favorite liquefied vegetables at the local market or juice bar. Using a vegetable broth is equally pleasing—choose a deeper, savory broth such as mushroom or beef-flavored vegan.

4 cups (940 ml) fresh green juice or low-sodium vegetable broth

1 teaspoon vegetable or extra-virgin olive oil

½ cup (80 g) diced onion

3 cloves garlic, minced

1 teaspoon ground rosemary

1 teaspoon coriander

1 teaspoon saffron strands

1 bay leaf

2 cups (400 g) dried split peas, rinsed and drained

2 cups (470 ml) water

Juice of 1 lemon

½ to 1 teaspoon sea salt (optional)

Ground black pepper

If you choose to use juice, make your favorite green juice. Mine is 2 golden beets, 5 kale leaves, 6 Swiss chard leaves, 1 cucumber, 1 zucchini, and 6 stalks of celery. This should make approximately 4 cups (940 ml) green juice; if not, add water to make up 4 cups (940 ml).

In an uncovered pressure cooker heat the oil on medium-high. Add the onion and garlic and sauté for 2 to 3 minutes, until the onion is soft. Add the rosemary, coriander, and saffron strands and stir well, covering the onion and garlic. Add the bay leaf, split peas, vegetable juice, and water. Stir to combine.

Cover and bring to pressure. Cook at high pressure for 6 minutes. Allow for a natural release.

Remove the bay leaf and stir in the lemon juice. Taste before adding salt. Serve with freshly ground pepper.

Yield: 6 servings

## Recipe Note

When cooking with saffron, a little goes a long way and that's great because it's expensive! You might not, however, experience its full flavor until the next day. This soup is great reheated for leftovers.

# Potato, Apple, and Lentil Soup

**Sometimes I make recipes simply based on what I have in the** refrigerator and pantry and similar cooking times. This is one of those recipes. I love apple and potato together. The apple adds a lightness to the soup and balances a heavy starch vegetable. And lentils are great in anything.

1 teaspoon extra-virgin olive oil

1 cup (160 g) diced onion

1 cup (130 g) chopped carrots

½ teaspoon chipotle powder

¼ teaspoon cayenne pepper

½ teaspoon ground cinnamon

3 cups (330 g) cubed potatoes

2 cups (300 g) diced apples

½ cup (100 g) dried brown lentils

4 cups (940 ml) low-sodium vegetable broth

½ to 1 teaspoon sea salt

Ground black pepper

In an uncovered pressure cooker, heat the oil on medium-high. Add the onion and carrots and sauté until the onions are soft, 3 to 4 minutes. Add the seasonings, potatoes, apples, lentils, and broth. Stir to combine.

Cover and bring to pressure. Cook at high pressure for 10 minutes. Allow for a natural release.

Remove the lid, taste and add salt to taste. Serve with freshly ground pepper.

Yield: 4 to 6 servings

# Tofu, Chickpea, Artichoke, and Potato Soup

In this recipe I use canned chickpeas because sometimes you want quick cooking even quicker. This soup is marvelous served over greens—such as sautéed collard greens—and garnished with capers.

1 large potato, diced

3 cloves garlic, minced

½ package (14 ounces, or 392 g) extra-firm tofu, pressed, drained, and diced

1 can (14 ounces, or 392 g) chickpeas, rinsed and drained

1 can (14 ounces, or 392 g) artichoke hearts, drained

1 tomato, diced

2 stalks celery, chopped

1 teaspoon paprika

1 teaspoon turmeric

5 cups (1.2 L) vegetable broth

¼ teaspoon ground black pepper

¼ cup (34 g) capers, for garnish

Place the potato, garlic, tofu, chickpeas, artichokes, tomato, celery, paprika, turmeric, and broth in the pressure cooker. Stir to combine.

Cover and bring to pressure. Cook at high pressure for 6 minutes. Use a quick release.

Serve with freshly ground pepper and capers (about 1 tablespoon [8.5 g] per bowl).

Yield: 4 servings

## Recipe Note

Save the other half of the tofu for a breakfast scramble or an "eggless" salad.

# Bean and Barley Stew

This dish is easily a one-pot meal because it is packed with everything
you need in a single sitting, but I still call it a stew because the mushrooms and barley add a soupy
thickness that demands a spoon. If you can't find baby bella mushrooms, try portobello or cremini.
Black, flageolet, or pinto beans are also terrific in place of the navy beans.

1 teaspoon extra-virgin olive oil

¼ cup (40 g) sliced shallot

2 stalks celery, diced

1 teaspoon seeded and
    minced fresh jalapeño

½ cup (35 g) sliced baby
    bella mushrooms

1 tomato, diced

1 cup (100 g) chopped
    green beans

1 bay leaf

1 teaspoon herbes de Provence

1 teaspoon dried thyme

1 teaspoon ground black pepper

4 cups (940 ml) low-sodium
    vegetable broth

3 cups (705 ml) water

1 cup (200 g) dried navy beans

¾ cup (150 g) dried pearl
    barley, rinsed and drained

Juice of 1 lemon

¼ teaspoon ground cardamom

½ to 1 teaspoon sea salt

In an uncovered pressure cooker, heat the oil on medium-high. Add the shallot, celery, and jalapeño and
sauté for 3 minutes, until the celery is soft. Add the
mushrooms, tomato, green beans, bay leaf, spices, broth,
water, beans, and barley. Stir to combine.

Cover and bring to pressure. Cook at high pressure for
20 to 22 minutes. Allow a natural release.

Remove the lid and stir in the lemon juice, cardamom,
and salt. If the beans are not quite done, simmer, uncovered, until cooked through. Remove the bay leaf before
serving.

Yield: 6 servings

# Vegan "Turkey," Bean, and Kale Soup

As an avid reader of food magazines and blogs, I have seen numerous turkey, kale, and white bean soup recipes. Already a lover of kale and beans, I decided to try a vegan version by using TVP—textured vegetable (soy) protein—as a ground meat replacement. This is very popular in my "multivore" home of one vegan and one omnivore.

1 teaspoon extra-virgin olive oil

½ cup (80 g) diced onion

2 tablespoons (20 g) minced garlic

1 cup (130 g) chopped carrots

1 cup (120 g) chopped celery

1 teaspoon ground cumin

1 teaspoon chili powder

1½ teaspoons dried oregano

1 tablespoon (8 g) chicken-flavored seasoning

½ cup (50 g) TVP

1 cup (200 g) dried Great Northern beans

4 cups (268 g) tightly packed kale, cut or torn into bite-size pieces

6 cups (1.4 L) low-sodium vegetable broth

4 cups (940 ml) water

2 tablespoons (32 g) tomato paste

2 tablespoons (30 ml) lemon juice

1 teaspoon sea salt

½ teaspoon ground black pepper

In an uncovered pressure cooker, heat the oil on medium-high. Add the onion and garlic and sauté for just 1 minute. Add the carrots and celery and sauté for another 2 to 3 minutes. Stir in the spices and chicken-flavored seasoning. Add the TVP, beans, kale, broth, and water. Stir to combine.

Cover and bring to pressure. Cook at high pressure for 25 to 30 minutes. Allow for a natural release.

Remove the lid and stir in the tomato paste, lemon juice, salt, and pepper. If the beans are not quite cooked through, simmer on low, with the pressure cooker uncovered, until done.

Yield: 4 servings

## Recipe Notes

- You may substitute water or broth for the oil.
- This soup is great served with something spicy such as Sriracha, Louisiana hot sauce, or diced jalapeño.
- Try Butler Foods, Frontier, or McKay's chicken-style seasoning.

# Anasazi Bean and Potato Soup

This colorful bean makes a far from ordinary potato soup! You may substitute pinto or cranberry beans for the anasazi beans, and/or regular potatoes for the fingerlings (though I love their creamy texture).

1 teaspoon extra-virgin olive oil

³/₄ cup (120 g) diced onion

3 cloves garlic, minced

2 tablespoons (18 g) diced jalapeño

¹/₂ teaspoon ground cumin

1 tablespoon (3 g) dried oregano

1 tablespoon (7 g) chili powder

1 teaspoon red pepper flakes

1 cup (150 g) diced yellow bell pepper

1¹/₂ cups (165 g) diced fingerling potatoes

2 cups (360 g) chopped fresh or canned diced tomatoes

¹/₂ teaspoon sea salt

2 bay leaves

6 cups (1.4 L) low-sodium vegetable broth

12 ounces (336 g) dried anasazi beans

2 tablespoons (30 ml) fresh lemon juice

In an uncovered pressure cooker, heat the oil on medium-high. Add the onion, garlic, jalapeño, cumin, oregano, chili powder, and red pepper flakes and sauté for 2 or 3 minutes. Add the bell pepper, potatoes, tomatoes, salt, bay leaves, vegetable broth, and beans. Stir to combine.

Cover and bring to pressure. Cook at low pressure for 22 to 25 minutes. Allow for a natural release.

Remove the lid, stir in the lemon juice, and do a taste test. If needed, add more salt. If the beans are not cooked through, simmer, uncovered, until done. Remove the bay leaves before serving.

Yield: 4 servings

## Recipe Note

If you soak the beans overnight this soup cooks up in 7 minutes!

# Speedy Bean Chili

**Sometimes even I don't have the time to cook dried beans. This is one** of my favorite chili recipes that, when cooked in the pressure cooker with canned or precooked beans, is done in 10 minutes! This chili is terrific served with a dollop of vegan sour cream.

1 teaspoon extra-virgin olive oil

1 cup (160 g) diced onion

3 cloves garlic, minced

1/2 cup (65 g) diced carrot

1/2 cup (60 g) chopped celery

1 cup (150 g) diced green bell pepper

1 cup (150 g) diced red bell pepper

1 seeded and finely diced fresh jalapeño

1/2 teaspoon cayenne pepper

1 teaspoon red pepper flakes

1 teaspoon chili powder

1/2 teaspoon ground cumin

1 can (28 ounces, or 784 g) diced tomatoes

2 tablespoons (36 g) tomato paste

2 cups (470 ml) low-sodium vegetable broth

1 cup (235 ml) water

1 can (14.5 ounces, or 406 g) whole kernel corn, drained

1 1/2 cups (375 g) red kidney beans (cooked or canned), rinsed and drained

1/2 to 1 teaspoon sea salt (optional)

In an uncovered pressure cooker, heat the oil on medium-high. Add the onion, garlic, carrot, and celery and sauté for 3 minutes. Add the bell peppers, jalapeño, cayenne, red pepper flakes, chili powder, cumin, diced tomatoes, tomato paste, broth, water, corn, and beans.

Cover and bring to pressure. Cook at low pressure for 6 minutes. Allow for a natural release.

Remove the lid, taste, and add salt, if desired.

Yield: 4 servings

## Recipe Note

Want to make this with a dried legume? Replace the cooked/canned kidney beans with dried brown lentils and cook for 10 minutes.

# Black Bean and Sweet Potato Stew

Black beans and sweet potatoes are visually appealing (we eat with our eyes first!) with their vibrant color, but they are also a dynamic nutrition duo: Black beans are rich in calcium, protein, potassium, and magnesium and sweet potatoes—a slow carb—is a lower glycemic index food that releases glucose gradually and is rich in beta-carotene. And they taste great together!

4 cups plus 2 tablespoons (970 ml) vegetable broth, divided

½ cup (80 g) chopped onion

4 cloves garlic, minced

2 carrots, chopped

1 large sweet potato, diced into equal, bite-size pieces

3 stalks celery, chopped

2 small tomatoes, diced

½ teaspoon ground cinnamon

1 teaspoon garam masala

1 cup (200 g) dried black beans, rinsed and drained

2 bay leaves

½ teaspoon sea salt (optional)

¼ teaspoon black pepper

In an uncovered pressure cooker, heat the 2 tablespoons (30 ml) vegetable broth on high. Add the onion and garlic and sauté for about 2 minutes, until the onion is soft. Add the carrots and sweet potato and sauté for another 3 minutes.

Add the celery, tomatoes, cinnamon, and garam masala and stir to coat all of the vegetables with the spices. Add the black beans, bay leaves, and remaining 4 cups (940 ml) vegetable broth. Stir to combine.

Cover and bring to pressure. Cook at high pressure for 22 to 24 minutes. Allow for a natural release.

Remove the lid, remove the bay leaves, stir in the salt and pepper, and serve.

Yield: 6 servings

# Kale, Lentil, and Squash Chili

It can be a challenge to rethink traditional chili of ground beef, red beans, and tomatoes. Kale and lentils are two of my favorite foods, and they go perfectly with squash, which makes for a creamy texture.

1 teaspoon vegetable oil

½ cup (80 g) diced onion

2 cloves garlic, minced

¼ cup (38 g) diced green bell pepper

3 cups (450 g) diced butternut squash (½-inch, or 1.3 cm cubes)

1½ teaspoons cumin

1 teaspoon chili powder

1 tablespoon (15 ml) Sriracha or other hot sauce

1 cup (200 g) dried brown lentils, rinsed and drained

2 tomatoes, diced

2 to 3 cups (470 to 705 ml) low-sodium vegetable broth, or more as needed

4 cups (268 g) loosely packed kale, cut or torn into bite-size pieces

1 tablespoon (15 ml) lemon juice

Salt and black pepper, to taste

In an uncovered pressure cooker, heat the oil on medium-high. Add the onion, garlic, and bell pepper and sauté for 2 to 3 minutes, until the onion softens. Add the squash, cumin, chili powder, and Sriracha and sauté for 3 to 5 minutes. Stir in the lentils and tomatoes.

Add enough vegetable broth to cover everything, then add more to cover by 1 inch (2.5 cm). Add the kale and stir to combine.

Cover and to bring to pressure. Cook at pressure for 8 to 10 minutes. Allow for a natural release.

Remove the lid. Return the uncovered pressure cooker back to low heat to simmer. Stir in the lemon juice. Add salt and ground black pepper to taste.

Yield: 6 servings

## Recipe Note

If you like your chili extra hot, consider adding jalapeño or habanero peppers.

# Flageolet Bean and Millet Stew

Flageolet beans are popular in French cuisine and particularly good in soups and salads. The green color of the beans, combined with a red apple and orange-hued millet, make for a colorful, rich stew.

1 ½ cups (300 g) dried flageolet beans, soaked for 12 hours or overnight

1 teaspoon extra-virgin olive oil

¼ cup sliced (40 g) shallot

½ cup (55 g) diced parsnip

1 gala or Red Delicious apple, diced

1 golden beet, diced

½ cup (80 g) millet

1 can (14 ounces, or 392 g) diced tomatoes

1 bay leaf

1 teaspoon whole fennel seed, crumbled

1 teaspoon dried thyme

1 teaspoon dried sweet basil

2 ½ cups (588 ml) vegetable broth, or more as needed

2 ½ cups (588 ml) water, or more as needed

1 to 2 tablespoons (15 to 30 ml) lemon juice

½ teaspoon sea salt (optional)

¼ to ½ teaspoon black pepper

Rinse and drain the beans.

In an uncovered pressure cooker, heat the oil on medium high. Add the shallot and sauté for just 1 minute, just to soften a bit. Add the parsnip, apple, and beet and sauté for 3 to 5 minutes. Add the beans, millet, diced tomatoes, bay leaf, fennel, thyme, and basil. Stir to combine.

Because you want a stewlike consistency, you want enough liquid to cook but not too much. Cover the vegetables and beans with a 50:50 mixture of broth and water. Once covered, add more so that there are 3 inches (7.5 cm) of liquid over the beans.

Cover and bring to pressure. Cook at high pressure 10 minutes. Allow for a natural release.

Remove the lid and stir in the lemon juice. Taste and determine how much salt is needed, if any. Remove the bay leaf before serving. Add ground pepper and serve.

Yield: 4 to 6 servings

# Chunky Red Lentil Stew

This very quick, thick stew is fantastic served over grains such as
barley, faro, or freekeh and is incredibly nutritious. Lentils are a good source of fiber, protein, iron,
calcium, zinc, and B vitamins and cooked tomatoes offer lycopene, a health-promoting antioxidant.

2 cups plus 2 tablespoons
(500 ml) vegetable broth,
divided

2 cloves garlic, minced

½ cup (80 g) diced yellow onion

2 carrots, chopped

½ teaspoon garam masala

½ teaspoon curry powder

1 tomato, cut into large chunks

1 cup (200 g) dried red lentils,
rinsed and drained

Juice of ½ lemon

Sea salt, to taste

In an uncovered pressure cooker, heat the 2 tablespoons
(30 ml) vegetable broth on high. Add the garlic and
onion and sauté for 2 to 3 minutes, until the onion is
soft. Stir in the carrots, garam masala, and curry powder
and sauté for another 2 to 3 minutes. Add the tomato,
lentils, and remaining 2 cups (470 ml) vegetable broth.
Stir to combine.

Cover and bring to pressure. Cook at high pressure for
6 minutes. Use a quick release.

Remove the lid and stir in the lemon juice, taste, and
add salt, as needed.

Yield: 4 servings

# Black-Eyed Pea and Collard Green Chili

**The combination of this legume and leafy green sounds like a typical**
Southern dish and understandably, because in the South it is considered good luck to consume together on New Year's Day. A colorful dish, the protein-rich black eyed pea and calcium-rich collard greens are also high in iron.

4 large collard green leaves

1 teaspoon extra-virgin olive oil

½ cup (80 g) diced red onion

3 cloves garlic, minced

2 cups (260 g) chopped carrot

2 cups (240 g) chopped celery

2 tablespoons (12 g) chili powder

1 teaspoon ground cumin

½ teaspoon ground coriander

1 teaspoon ground cinnamon

1 tablespoon (3 g) dried oregano

1 teaspoon seeded and diced fresh jalapeño

2 cups (400 g) dried black-eyed peas, rinsed and drained

2 bay leaves

1 can (28 ounces, or 784 g) diced tomatoes

1 can (8 ounces, or 224 g) tomato sauce

2 cups (470 ml) vegetable broth

1 cup (235 ml) water

¼ to ½ teaspoon sea salt (optional)

Halve each collard leaf lengthwise with kitchen shears or a sharp knife, cutting out and discarding the center ribs. Stack the leaves and cut crosswise into ¼-inch (6 mm) wide strips.

In an uncovered pressure cooker heat the oil on medium-high. Add the onion and garlic and sauté for about 2 minutes, until the onion begins to soften. Add the carrots and celery and continue to sauté for another 3 to 5 minutes. Add the collard greens, chili powder, cumin, coriander, cinnamon, oregano, and jalapeño and sauté for a minute or two. Add the black-eyed peas, bay leaves, diced tomatoes, tomato sauce, broth, and water. Stir to combine.

Cover and bring to pressure. Cook at high pressure for 10 minutes. Allow for a natural release.

Remove the cover and taste the black-eyed peas. Add salt to taste. If they are not thoroughly cooked, simmer on low, uncovered, until done. Remove the bay leaves before serving.

Yield: 4 to 6 servings

# Asian Adzuki Bean Chili

The first time I used adzuki beans I researched them and learned that they are popular in Japanese cuisine. This inspired me to think about other Eastern-influenced flavors and seasoning to make a different kind of chili.

1 1/2 cups (300 g) dried adzuki beans, soaked for 12 hours or overnight

1 tablespoon (15 ml) sesame oil

3 or 4 large cloves garlic, minced

1 cup (160 g) diced onion

1 cup (130 g) chopped carrots

4 cups (940 ml) vegetable broth

1 can (14 ounces, or 392 g) fire-roasted diced tomatoes

2 tablespoons (32 g) tomato paste

1 teaspoon Herbamare

1 teaspoon dulse flakes

1 tablespoon (15 ml) yuzu pepper sauce

1 tablespoon (15 ml) low-sodium soy sauce

2 cups (180 g) sliced cabbage

Rinse and drain the beans.

In an uncovered pressure cooker, heat the oil on medium heat. Add the garlic, onion, and carrots and sauté for 3 minutes, until the onion is soft. Add the broth, beans, tomatoes, tomato paste, Herbamare, dulse, pepper sauce, soy sauce, and cabbage. Stir to combine.

Cover and bring to pressure. Cook at high pressure for 7 minutes. Allow for a natural release.

Yield: 6 servings

## Recipe Notes

• Herbamare and dulse flakes (a sea vegetable) are salt alternatives with an Asian flare. Dulse flakes can be found in the Asian section of the grocery store; if you can't find them, try wakame, arame, or hijiki (other types of sea vegetables).

• Yuzu pepper sauce is a Japanese hot sauce; you can substitute your favorite hot sauce.

# Summer Lentil and Millet Chili

This chili pulls together what I consider to be the three vegan meal essentials: beans, greens, and grains. Summer vegetables fresh from the garden and light lentils with quick-to-cook millet make this chili perfect in the summer, no matter how hot the day.

2 tablespoons (30 ml) olive oil

1 cup (160 g) finely diced yellow onion

2 cloves garlic, minced

1 seeded and finely diced fresh jalapeño

½ teaspoon ground cinnamon

1 teaspoon chili powder

1 teaspoon ground cumin

1 bay leaf

½ cup (60 g) diced summer squash (lightly peeled, if needed)

4 cups (720 g) diced fresh tomatoes

2 cups (134 g) tightly packed bite-size pieces kale

1 cup (200 g) dried brown lentils, rinsed and drained

1 cup (88 g) millet, rinsed and drained

2 cups (470 ml) low-sodium vegetable broth

4 cups (940 ml) water

Juice of 1 lemon

1 tablespoon (2 g) chopped fresh sweet basil, plus more for garnish

½ teaspoon sea salt, or to taste

Heat the olive oil in a 6-quart (6 L) or larger pressure cooker (if your pressure cooker is smaller, reduce the quantity of chili by half). Add the onion and cook for 3 to 4 minutes, stirring occasionally, until softened. Add the garlic, stir, then add the jalapeño, cinnamon, chili powder, and cumin and sauté for a few minutes more, until the jalapeño softens. Add the bay leaf, squash, tomatoes, kale, lentils, millet, broth, and water and stir to combine.

Cover and bring to high pressure (this will take a while because the pressure cooker is loaded with veggies, lentils, grains, and liquid). Once high pressure is achieved, lower the heat to maintain pressure. Cook at pressure for 8 minutes. Remove from the burner and allow for a natural release.

Once the pressure is released, carefully remove the lid, pointing it away from you. Place back on the burner, uncovered, on low heat and bring to a simmer, then add the lemon juice, basil, and salt.

Stir and let simmer for a few minutes more. Garnish with additional fresh basil.

Yield: 6 to 8 servings

# CHAPTER FOUR

# One-Pot Meals

Raise your hand if you bought your pressure cooker because you wanted to make one-pot meals? My hand is raised! Although I love using my rice and slow cookers, I am constantly seduced by the speed of a pressure cooker. These meals are done in minutes, yet taste like they've been cooking for hours!

# Black Beans and Quinoa

This one-pot meal is great as an entrée served over raw or sautéed greens, and it also makes a great side dish with grilled or baked tofu or tempeh. Try it cold as a filling wrapped in raw collard greens or in a tortilla wrap sandwich.

1 cup (200 g) dried black beans, soaked for 12 hours or overnight

1 cup (130 g) diced carrot

¼ cup (40 g) diced sweet onion

1 clove garlic, minced

1 ½ cups (265 g) quinoa

1 teaspoon chili powder

2 cups (470 ml) low-sodium vegetable broth

½ teaspoon sea salt (optional)

Add all the ingredients to the pressure cooker. Stir to combine. Cover and bring to pressure. Cook at high pressure for 6 minutes. Allow for a natural release.

Yield: 4 servings

# Navy Beans, Rice, and Greens

Another simple beans, greens, and grains recipe—this time with quick-cooking rice and calcium-rich kale—that is filling and cooks up in no time. Serve as an entrée and use the leftovers as a side dish for another meal.

1 cup (200 g) dried navy beans, soaked for 12 hours or overnight

1 teaspoon vegetable oil

½ cup (80 g) diced red onion

3 cloves garlic, minced

½ cup (95 g) short-grain white rice

4 cups (280 g) loosely packed bite-size pieces kale

1 bay leaf

1 teaspoon dried thyme

2½ cups (588 ml) water, or more as needed

1 tablespoon (15 ml) lemon juice

½ to 1 teaspoon sea salt

Rinse and drain the beans.

In an uncovered pressure cooker, heat the oil on medium-high. Add the onion and garlic and sauté for 3 minutes, until the onion is soft. Add the beans, rice, kale, bay leaf, thyme, and water to cover.

Cover and bring to pressure. Cook at high pressure for 6 to 8 minutes. Allow for a natural release.

Remove the lid, remove and discard the bay leaf, and stir in the lemon juice and salt.

Yield: 4 servings

## Recipe Notes

- If you don't have time to soak the navy beans, proceed with the dried beans, increase the water by ½ cup (120 ml), and cook for 22 minutes total.

- For a leafy green alternative, substitute baby spinach or shredded collard greens for the kale.

# New World Székely Goulash

Early in our marriage, my half-Hungarian husband introduced me to "old world" goulash made with sauerkraut, pork, and sour cream. This was foreign to me, the girl who was raised in rural Illinois and knew goulash as elbow macaroni, ground beef, and tomatoes. This recipe is a blend of the traditional Székely goulash ingredients—specifically the sauerkraut and sour cream—with the Midwest addition of tomatoes. The chickpeas stand in as the protein replacement for the pork.

1 cup (200 g) dried chickpeas, soaked for 12 hours or overnight

1 teaspoon extra-virgin olive oil

2 cloves garlic, minced

1/2 cup (80 g) half-moon slices yellow onion

1 1/2 cups (195 g) chopped carrots

2 tablespoons (14 g) paprika, plus more for garnish

1 teaspoon freshly ground black pepper, plus more for serving

2 cups (470 ml) vegetable broth

1 cup (245 g) tomato sauce

1 bay leaf

1 to 1 1/2 cups (235 to 355 ml) water, or as needed

1 teaspoon sea salt

32 ounces (896 g) sauerkraut, drained

1/2 cup (120 g) vegan sour cream

Rinse and drain the chickpeas.

In an uncovered pressure cooker, heat the olive oil on medium-high heat. Add the garlic, onion, and carrots and sauté for 3 minutes, until the onion softens. Stir in the paprika and black pepper. Add the chickpeas, vegetable broth, tomato sauce, bay leaf, and enough water to cover everything, plus an additional 1/2 inch (1.3 cm).

Cover and bring to pressure. Cook at high pressure for 13 to 15 minutes. Allow for a natural release.

Remove the cover and stir in the salt. If the chickpeas are not quite done, simmer on low until thoroughly cooked. Remove and discard the bay leaf.

Stir in the sauerkraut and vegan sour cream and simmer on low until everything is completely heated through. Garnish with a dash of paprika and serve with freshly ground black pepper.

Yield: 6 servings

# Quinoa-Millet-Pea Bowl

This recipe is lightly seasoned to allow the contrasting textures of the peas, grains, and vegetables to come through. Rosemary offers a hint of seasoning to this light yet substantial meal.

½ cup (100 g) dried whole peas, soaked for 12 hours or overnight

½ cup (60 g) sliced zucchini

½ cup (60 g) chopped celery

¼ cup (40 g) finely diced onion

1 cup (175 g) quinoa, rinsed and drained

½ cup (90 g) millet, rinsed and drained

2 cups (470 ml) vegetable broth

½ to 1 cup (120 to 235 ml) water

1 teaspoon whole rosemary, crumbled

½ to 1 teaspoon sea salt

Rinse and drain the peas. Place all the ingredients, except the salt, in the pressure cooker. Stir to combine.

Cover and bring to pressure. Cook at high pressure for 8 to 10 minutes. Allow for a natural release.

Remove the lid and stir in the salt to taste. Fluff up the millet with a fork. Leave uncovered for about 5 minutes, then fluff again before serving.

Yield: 4 to 6 servings

## Recipe Note

Adzuki, Great Northern, or kidney beans are good substitutes for peas if you want to add more protein to this dish.

# Amaranth Lentils

I consider this a power dish—or is it a power bowl? It's packed with protein, fiber, iron, calcium, magnesium, and more! Nutrient-dense, the texture is nice and light.

1 teaspoon vegan butter

2 cloves garlic, minced

¼ cup (40 g) diced yellow onion

½ cup (100 g) amaranth

½ cup (100 g) dried brown lentils

2 cups (140 g) shredded Swiss chard

2 to 2¼ cups (470 to 530 ml) water, or as needed

¼ teaspoon ground coriander

½ teaspoon sea salt

¼ cup (25 g) chopped scallion

In an uncovered pressure cooker, melt the butter on medium heat. Add the garlic and onion and sauté until the onion is soft, about 3 minutes. Add the amaranth, lentils, and Swiss chard and stir to combine. Add the water: Start with 2 cups (470 ml) water and add enough to cover everything. Stir to combine.

Cover and bring to pressure. Cook at high pressure for 8 to 10 minutes. Allow for a natural release.

Remove the cover and stir in the coriander and salt. Garnish with the scallion.

Yield: 4 servings

## Recipe Note

Collard greens, turnip greens, and kale are all great substitutes for Swiss chard.

# Black Beans and Yams

Why use canned beans in the pressure cooker? Because sometimes you forget to cook your beans and you *still* want dinner in less than 10 minutes! Serve these black beans and yams over a bed of arugula or sautéed kale to get your leafy greens!

2 cups (220 g) diced yams

1 cup (235 ml) vegetable broth

1/2 cup (130 g) salsa (jarred, fresh, or homemade)

1 can (14 ounces, or 392 g) black beans, rinsed and drained

Add all the ingredients to the pressure cooker. Cover and bring to pressure. Cook at high pressure for 4 minutes. Use a quick release.

Yield: 2 to 4 servings

# Gingered Adzuki Beans, Greens, and Grains

Inspired by Lorna Sass's Gingered Adzuki Squash Stew recipe, this is a one-pot hippie bowl meal!

1 teaspoon sesame oil

2 or 3 cloves garlic, minced

1 teaspoon grated ginger

1/2 cup (35 g) sliced maitake or shiitake mushrooms

2 cups (140 g) shredded collard greens, Swiss chard, kale, or a mix

1 cup (200 g) dried adzuki beans

1/2 cup (95 g) brown rice

1-inch (2.5 cm) strip kombu

3 cups (705 ml) water

3 umeboshi plums, mashed with a fork

1 tablespoon (15 ml) lemon juice

1 tablespoon (15 ml) tamari

In an uncovered pressure cooker, heat the oil on medium-high. Add the garlic and ginger and sauté for 2 minutes, until the garlic is softened. Stir in the mushrooms, greens, adzuki beans, brown rice, kombu, and water.

Cover and bring to pressure. Cook at high pressure for 22 minutes. Allow for a natural release.

Remove the cover and stir. Return to the burner, turn the heat to low, and simmer while stirring in the mashed umeboshi plums, lemon juice, and tamari (about 3 minutes).

Yield: 4 to 6 servings

# Vegan "Bacon" and Cabbage

I had a vegetarian "oops" moment years ago in Ireland. I ordered the cabbage and, unbeknownst to me, bacon is a standard ingredient in their version. Since then, I've created a simple, plant-based version that cooks up quickly and is sure to wow your omnivore friends and family.

||||||||||||||||||||||||||||||||||||||||||||||||||||||||||||||||||||||||||||||||||||||||||||||||||||||||||||||||||||||||

4 tablespoons (55 g) vegan butter

1 package (5 ounces, or 140 g) vegan bacon, cut into $\frac{1}{2}$-inch (1.3 cm) pieces

1 sweet onion, cut into half-moon slices

2 potatoes, peeled and diced into bite-size cubes

1 head cabbage, cored and thinly sliced (about 1 $\frac{1}{2}$ pounds, or 680 g)

1 tablespoon (7 g) smoked paprika

1 $\frac{1}{2}$ cups (355 ml) vegan chicken-flavored broth

Salt and freshly ground black pepper, to taste

In an uncovered pressure cooker, melt the butter on medium-high. Add the bacon pieces and stir well to cover with the butter. Add the onion and sauté until soft, about 3 minutes. Add the potatoes, cabbage, and paprika. Add the broth and stir to combine.

Cover and bring to pressure. Cook at high pressure for 4 minutes. Allow for a natural release.

Remove the cover and add salt and pepper to taste.

Yield: 6 servings

## Recipe Notes

• Because vegan bacon will not have "drippings," vegan butter adds liquid to the sauté process. You can substitute 1 to 2 tablespoons (15 to 30 ml) extra-virgin olive oil or $\frac{1}{4}$ to $\frac{1}{2}$ cup (60 to 120 ml) vegetable broth.

• You can find vegan chicken-flavored broth at many grocery stores, or heat 1 $\frac{1}{2}$ cups (355 ml) water with vegan chicken-flavored bouillon.

# Korean Kongbap

Kongbap is a Korean dish comprising white or brown rice cooked with one or more beans (and sometimes also other grains). This basic recipe is true to the traditional dish—beans and grains with no spices, though I do use sesame oil for both flavor and to avoid possible foaming. Serve this over a bed of sautéed greens with soy sauce and a garnish of freshly grated ginger, as a side dish with a generous helping of your favorite hot sauce, such as Sriracha, or as an appetizer rolled up in a nori sheet for a Korean kongbap sushi roll—just dip in soy sauce with wasabi.

½ cup (100 g) dried
    black soybeans

½ cup (100 g) dried whole peas

½ cup (95 g) brown rice

½ cup (100 g) pearl barley

7 to 7 ½ cups (1.6 to 1.8 L) water,
    divided

1 tablespoon (15 ml) sesame oil

Combine the soybeans, peas, brown rice, and pearl barley to a large bowl and add 4 cups (940 ml) of the water. Soak overnight.

Rinse, drain, and add to the pressure cooker. Add the remaining 3 to 3 ½ cups (705 to 825 ml) water. Drizzle the oil over the water. Stir to combine.

Cover and bring to pressure. Cook at high pressure for 22 minutes. Allow for a natural release; if after 10 minutes the pressure has still not come down fully, manually release.

Yield: 6 servings

## Recipe Note

This is the consummate bulk-cooked recipe—you can add it to soups, salads, stir-fries, and more.

# Lentil, Kale, and Barley Risotto

This longer cooking risotto features pearl barley. The first time I made this dish I was deep into half-marathon training and this was my go-to "carbo-load" meal. Serve this as an entrée or as a side dish with baked tofu. Please note that this calls for cooked lentils, which you can make in advance.

4 teaspoons (20 ml) extra-virgin olive oil

¼ cup (40 g) diced onion

2 cloves garlic, minced

1 teaspoon seeded and diced fresh jalapeño

1 cup (200 g) dried pearl barley

2 cups (470 ml) vegetable broth, or more as needed

1 cup (235 ml) water, or more as needed

¼ teaspoon sea salt, plus more to taste

¼ teaspoon black pepper, plus more to taste

2 cups (340 g) cooked lentils

2 cups (140 g) tightly packed chopped kale

2 to 3 tablespoons (30 to 45 ml) lemon juice

¼ cup (24 g) nutritional yeast

2 teaspoons grated vegan Parmesan cheese

1 teaspoon dried sweet basil

In an uncovered pressure cooker, heat the oil on medium-high. Add the onion, garlic, and jalapeño and sauté for 3 minutes, until the onion is soft. Add the barley, vegetable broth, water, salt, and pepper. Stir to combine.

Cover and bring to pressure. Cook at high pressure for 18 to 20 minutes. Use a quick release.

Remove the lid and stir in the cooked lentils, kale, lemon juice, nutritional yeast, Parmesan cheese, and basil. Simmer on low for approximately 10 minutes or to the desired risotto consistency (add more vegetable broth or water if needed). Taste and season with salt and pepper.

Yield: 6 to 8 servings

# Fava Bean Risotto

I include two risotto recipes in this book, and both contain legumes. This recipe is excellent with or without a legume, but as a one-pot meal, the addition of fresh fava beans provides an inexpensive lean protein element to the dish.

1 tablespoon (14 g) vegan butter

3 cloves garlic, minced

¼ cup (40 g) diced onion

¼ cup (18 g) diced mushrooms

1 cup (125 g) fresh fava beans

1 cup (125 g) Arborio rice

2 cups (470 ml) vegetable broth

1¼ cups (295 ml) water

2 tablespoons (10 g) grated vegan Parmesan cheese

2 tablespoons (14 g) nutritional yeast

½ to 1 teaspoon sea salt

In an uncovered pressure cooker melt the butter on medium-high. Add the garlic and onion and sauté for 3 minutes, until the onion is soft. Add the mushrooms, fava beans, and rice and stir to cover with the butter. Add the vegetable broth and water. Stir to combine.

Cover and bring to pressure. Cook at high pressure for 7 minutes. Use a quick release.

Remove the cover and stir in the Parmesan cheese, nutritional yeast, and salt to taste.

Yield: 4 servings

# Black-Eyed Peas and Farro

**Black-eyed peas and collard greens, when eaten on New Year's Day,** are said to bring great fortune. True or not, they are a culinary match made in heaven. The first time I made this dish I rolled it up in large, raw collard green leaves (a crunchy, healthy alternative to a tortilla wrap), but it's also great over sautéed collard green strips.

2 tablespoons (30 ml) extra-virgin olive oil

1/2 cup (80 g) diced yellow onion

3 cloves garlic, chopped

2/3 cup (132 g) farro, rinsed

1/2 teaspoon crumbled dried thyme leaves

1/2 teaspoon dried sweet basil

3/4 cup (150 g) dried black-eyed peas

1 cup (235 ml) low-sodium vegetable broth

1 cup (235 ml) water

1 tablespoon (15 ml) soy sauce, tamari, or Bragg Liquid Aminos

1/2 teaspoon Sriracha or other hot sauce

In an uncovered pressure cooker, heat the oil on medium-high. Add the onion and garlic and sauté for 3 minutes, until the onion is translucent. Stir in the farro, thyme, and basil, then add the black-eyed peas, broth, and water. Stir to combine.

Cover and bring to pressure, then reduce the heat to maintain pressure. Cook at pressure for 10 minutes. Allow for a natural release.

Remove the lid and stir in the soy sauce and Sriracha.

Yield: 4 servings

# Soy Curl Mac 'n Cheese

Soy curls, a textured vegetable protein food, are used in place of chicken in dishes such as stir-fries, casseroles, tacos, salads, and more. In this quick and easy vegan version of macaroni and cheese, the legume meat substitute adds protein, flavor, and density to a memorable comfort food.

This dish is fantastic with just the nutritional yeast, but if you're looking for something "cheesier," perhaps to impress non-vegan friends or family, stir in your favorite vegan cheese.

2 cups (200 g) soy curls

2 cups (470 ml) warm water plus 2 cups (470 ml) cold water, or more as needed, divided

2 tablespoons (28 g) vegan butter

1 cup (160 g) diced onion

2 cloves garlic, minced

2 tablespoons (16 g) vegan chicken-flavored seasoning

1/4 to 1/2 teaspoon black pepper

1 cup (105 g) spelt elbow pasta

2 tablespoons (14 g) nutritional yeast

1/2 to 1 teaspoon salt

2 ounces (56 g) shredded vegan cheese (optional)

Rehydrate the soy curls by placing them in a large bowl and cover with the 2 cups (470 ml) warm water. Let sit for 10 minutes. Drain the excess liquid and set aside.

In an uncovered pressure cooker, heat the butter on medium-high. Add the onion and garlic and sauté for 3 minutes, until the onion is translucent. Stir in the soy curls, chicken-flavored seasoning, and pepper. Sauté for about 5 minutes. If the soy curls begin to stick to the pressure cooker, add 1 tablespoon (15 ml) water or vegetable broth.

Add the pasta and remaining 2 cups (470 ml) cold water, or as needed to cover the pasta. Stir in the nutritional yeast, and pat the soy curls and pasta down under the water.

Cover and bring to pressure. Cook at low pressure for 5 minutes. Use a quick release.

Remove the lid and taste before adding salt. Add the cheese and mix well. Let stand for 5 minutes to allow it to set up for a firmer consistency before serving.

Yield: 2 servings

## Recipe Note

You can try other whole-grain pasta varieties; just make sure the cooking times listed on the package are similar to that of the spelt.

# Seitan Swiss Steak

## Swiss steak made the dinner rotation when I was growing up.

I often tell people that going vegan doesn't mean we no longer like what we used to eat—we just want a healthier, more compassionate choice. This recipe really grabs all of the elements I recall: the smell of the browning food, the thickness of the tomato gravy, and the need to eat it with mashed potatoes.

3 heaping tablespoons (24 g) flour

1 teaspoon salt

1/4 teaspoon black pepper

4 seitan cutlets (page 146) or 1 package (8 ounces, or 224 g) prepared seitan strips

1/4 cup (60 ml) extra-virgin olive oil

1 cup (160 g) half-moon slices yellow onion

1/2 cup (60 g) chopped celery

1 can (15 ounces, or 420 g) diced tomatoes

1/2 teaspoon vegan Worcestershire sauce

Mix the flour, salt, and pepper on a plate and dredge both sides of each seitan cutlet in the flour. Set aside.

In an uncovered pressure cooker, heat the oil on medium-high. Add the floured seitan and brown for 2 1/2 minutes, then turn over and brown for another 2 1/2 minutes. Transfer the browned seitan to a plate and set aside.

Add 1 tablespoon (8 g) leftover flour mix to the oil and seitan drippings remaining in the pressure cooker. Whisk until thickened. Add the onion, celery, tomatoes, and Worcestershire sauce. This should bubble from the heat right away. Stir well. Place the browned seitan back into the pressure cooker. Gently spoon the tomato gravy over the cutlets.

Cover and bring to pressure. Cook at high pressure for 2 minutes. Use a quick release. Remove the lid and serve immediately.

Yield: 4 servings

## Recipe Note

Traditional Worcestershire sauce contains anchovies; if you cannot find a vegan version, substitute with steak sauce mixed with a little soy sauce to thin it out.

# Tofu Scramble

## Why, you ask? Why make a tofu scramble in the pressure cooker

when you can make it in a skillet fairly quickly? One word: lazy. If you want to get everything going, walk away, and just come back to eat, this one's for you!

¾ cup (180 ml) vegetable broth, divided

3 carrots, diced

2 stalks celery, chopped

½ cup (80 g) diced yellow onion

1 block (14 ounces, or 392 g) firm or extra-firm tofu, pressed and drained

1 teaspoon turmeric

½ teaspoon garlic salt

½ teaspoon chili powder

2 cups (140 g) tightly packed bite-size pieces kale

½ teaspoon sea salt (optional)

In an uncovered pressure cooker, heat ½ cup (120 ml) of the vegetable broth on medium-high. Add the carrots, celery, and onion and sauté until most of the vegetable broth is absorbed, about 3 minutes.

Crumble the tofu with your hands into the pressure cooker. You want the tofu texture to resemble scrambled eggs. Add the turmeric, garlic salt, and chili powder and stir well. Stir in the kale. Pour the remaining ¼ cup (60 ml) vegetable broth over the scramble.

Cover and bring to pressure. Cook at high pressure for 4 minutes. Use a quick release.

Remove the lid, stir in the salt to taste, and serve.

Yield: 4 servings

CHAPTER FIVE

# Meal Helpers and Veggie Sides

By now you see that the pressure cooker is great for making bean and grain staples, soups and stews, and one-pot meals. It's a terrific tool to help get quick meals on the table. The recipes in this chapter range from meal helpers to side dishes to make your time in the kitchen quick and delicious.

# Rosemary and Thyme Brussels Sprouts

**Brussels sprouts are quite possible one of my favorite vegetables—** they are delicious and they are a terrific source of calcium and magnesium, which are great for bone health. I opt for the pressure cooker when I don't have the time (or patience) to roast my beloved sprouts.

1 pound (454 g) Brussels sprouts

1 teaspoon whole rosemary leaves

1 teaspoon dried thyme leaves

1 tablespoon (15 ml) walnut oil

1 tablespoon (10 g) coarsely chopped garlic

¼ teaspoon sea salt

1 cup (235 ml) water

1 teaspoon balsamic vinegar (optional)

Wash the brussels sprouts and remove the stems with a knife; the loose outer leaves should come off easily. Cut each in half. Set aside.

Crumble the rosemary and thyme with a mortar and pestle or by rubbing between you thumb and forefinger. Set aside.

In an uncovered pressure cooker, heat the oil on medium-high. Add the garlic and stir, coating with oil. Add the Brussels sprouts and sauté on medium heat for 5 minutes, stirring frequently. The sprouts will begin to turn a light brown (add a teaspoon or two of water if the garlic or sprouts stick to the pan). Add the rosemary, thyme, salt, and water.

Cover and bring to pressure. Cook at high pressure for 1 minute. Use a quick release.

Remove the lid, stir in the balsamic vinegar, and serve immediately.

Yield: 4 servings

## Recipe Note

Substitute extra-virgin olive oil or ¼ cup (60 ml) vegetable broth for the walnut oil.

# Turnips and Tomatoes
# over Freekeh

Many people turn their nose up to turnips because they find the
taste bitter and—most likely—because they just haven't had them prepared well. Combining tomatoes and maple syrup with turnips makes for a tangy and sweet taste that complements a hearty
grain, such as freekeh (see page 36).

1 teaspoon extra-virgin olive oil

1 cup (160 g) diced onion

1 ½ tablespoons (15 g) minced
    garlic

4 cups (600 g) peeled and
    diced turnip

3 cups (540 g) diced fresh
    tomato

1 tablespoon (8 g) freshly
    grated ginger

1 teaspoon ground cardamom

1 teaspoon ground coriander

1 teaspoon ground cumin

½ teaspoon turmeric powder

1 tablespoon (15 ml) maple syrup

1 tablespoon (15 ml) lime juice

1 cup (235 ml) vegetable broth

½ teaspoon sea salt

1 recipe Freekeh, (see page 36)

Add all the ingredients except the salt to the pressure
cooker. Cover and bring to pressure. Cook at high pressure for 10 minutes. Use a quick release. Remove the
cover, stir in the salt, and serve over the freekeh.

Yield: 4 servings

# Almond Garlic Green Beans

## I took one of my favorite ways to prepare vegetables—stir-frying

them in a little oil and with lots of garlic—and adapted it to the pressure cooker for a super-fast, flavor-infused steamed dish. When cooking vegetables, remember to use a quick release to avoid a mushy result.

1 teaspoon sesame oil

4 or 5 cloves garlic, thinly sliced lengthwise

1 pound (454 g) green beans, cut into ½-inch (1.3 cm) pieces

¼ cup (60 ml) water

¼ teaspoon sea salt

¼ cup (27 g) almond slivers

In an uncovered pressure cooker, heat the oil on medium. Add the garlic and sauté until soft, about 2 minutes.
Add the green beans and water.
    Cover and bring to pressure. Cook at pressure for 1 minute. Use a quick release.
    Remove the lid stir in the salt. Add the almond slivers, toss, and serve.

Yield: 4 servings

## Recipe Note

Substitute sesame oil with olive oil or ¼ cup (60 ml) water or vegetable broth.

# Lemony Artichokes
# with Horseradish Butter

**Artichokes are a vegetable I love, but I usually buy them already** cooked in a can or frozen. Enter the pressure cooker! With little preparation beyond trimming, the artichoke cooks up in less than 10 minutes and is ready to chop and add to a salad or to dip in your favorite sauce (mine is below).

2 medium artichokes

Juice of 1 lemon

4 tablespoons (56 g)
   vegan butter

½ teaspoon horseradish
   powder

Place a trivet in the pressure cooker, place a steamer basket on top of the trivet, and add enough water to come up to, but not in, the basket. Bring the water to a boil.

While the water heats, trim the base of each artichoke with a knife. If you like, you can also remove the sharp points of the leaves with kitchen shears. Add the artichokes and lemon juice to the pressure cooker.

Cover and bring to pressure. Cook at high pressure for 6 to 8 minutes. Use a quick release.

While the artichokes are cooking, heat the vegan butter in the microwave or in a saucepan. Whisk in the horseradish powder and set aside.

Remove the lid and use tongs to remove the steamer basket. Use the tongs to place the artichokes on a plate. Serve with the horseradish butter by dipping each leaf in the butter and sucking out the artichoke meat.

Yield: 2 servings

# Steamed Kabocha Squash

**Known as the Japanese pumpkin, kabocha squash is wonderful to**
have on hand to add to soups, to reheat and mash, and to add to cold salads.

**1 kabocha squash**

Place a trivet in the pressure cooker, place a steamer basket on top of the trivet, and add enough water to come up to, but not in, the basket. Bring the water to a boil.

Wash the kabocha squash well, as the skin is edible. Cut in half and scoop out the seeds. Place the squash in the steamer basket, cut-side up.

Cover and bring to pressure. Cook at high pressure for 4 minutes. Allow for a natural release; if after 10 minutes the pressure has still not come down fully, manually release.

Serve immediately, store in an airtight container in the refrigerator for 3 to 4 days, or freeze in a sturdy bag for 6 to 8 months.

Yield: 4 servings

# Bok Choy, Mushrooms, and Onion with Tamari Lime Dressing

Bok choy, a member of the cabbage family, is packed with vitamins A and C. Cooked up quickly with mushroom and onion, this wholesome side dish—served with an umami (see page 25) dressing—delivers a whole lot of flavor.

## FOR VEGETABLES:

5 to 6 cups (450 to 540 g) chopped bok choy

2 ½ cups (175 g) sliced shiitake, cremini, or maitake mushrooms

1 cup (160 g) half-moon slices onion

¼ teaspoon salt (optional)

## FOR DRESSING:

½ cup (120 ml) tamari

1 teaspoon minced garlic

½ teaspoon red pepper flakes

2 tablespoons (30 ml) lime juice

**To make the vegetables:** Place a trivet in the pressure cooker, place a steamer basket on top of the trivet, and add enough water to come up to, but not in, the basket. Bring the water to a boil. Place the bok choy, mushrooms, and onion in the basket. Sprinkle a pinch of salt over the vegetables if you are not planning on serving with the dressing.

Cover and bring to pressure. Cook at low pressure for 5 minutes. Use a quick release.

Remove the lid, use tongs to remove the steamer basket, and carefully spoon the vegetables into a bowl.

**To make the dressing:** Whisk the dressing ingredients together in a bowl. Pour over the vegetables in the bowl, toss lightly, and serve immediately.

Yield: 4 servings

# Root Veggie Tagine

Tagine is a North African stew, typically made of spiced meat and vegetables in a shallow cooking dish. No meat here, and my cooking dish is the pressure cooker. This dish is packed with spices and flavor. Serve it with the Cinnamon-Curried Chickpeas on page 23 and couscous or other grains such as barley or freekeh for a rich meal.

2 cups (220 g) diced sweet pota-toes (¹/₂-inch, or 1.3 cm cubes)

2 cups (240 g) diced carrots (¹/₂-inch, or 1.3 cm)

1 cup (150 g) cubed turnips (¹/₂-inch, or 1.3 cm)

¹/₂ teaspoon ground ginger

¹/₂ teaspoon ground cumin

¹/₂ teaspoon ground cinnamon

¹/₂ teaspoon saffron strands

1 teaspoon sugar

¹/₂ cup (120 ml) orange juice

¹/₂ cup (120 ml) water

¹/₂ teaspoon sea salt

Place all the ingredients in the pressure cooker. Stir well, covering the vegetables with the orange juice and water. Cover and bring to pressure. Cook at high pressure for 3 to 4 minutes. Use a quick release. Remove the lid, stir, and serve.

Yield: 4 to 6 servings

# Veggie Stewed Tomatoes

## This is a great staple to keep in the refrigerator or freezer to add to

dishes that require diced or stewed tomatoes. I mix these with cooked elbow macaroni for a Midwestern-style goulash or use them to top a bowl of cooked beans, greens, and grains.

1 tablespoon (15 ml) olive oil

2 cloves garlic, minced

1 cup (160 g) diced onion

½ cup (65 g) chopped carrot

½ cup (60 g) chopped celery

4 cups (600 g) quartered tomatoes

1 tablespoon (2 g) dried basil

1 tablespoon (3 g) dried oregano

1 tablespoon (1.5 g) dried parsley

1 teaspoon red pepper flakes

1 teaspoon salt

½ cup (120 ml) water

2 to 3 tablespoons (32 to 48 g) tomato paste (optional)

Ground black pepper

In an uncovered pressure cooker, heat the oil on medium-high. Add the garlic, onion, carrot, and celery and sauté for about 3 minutes, until the onion is soft. Add the tomatoes, basil, oregano, parsley, red pepper flakes, salt, and water and mix well.

Cover and bring to pressure. Cook at high pressure for 5 minutes. Use a quick release.

Remove the lid. With a potato masher, crush the tomatoes. If a thicker consistency is desired, stir in the tomato paste and simmer, uncovered, for about 5 minutes. Add the ground black pepper to taste.

Yield: 4 cups (980 g)

## Recipe Note

These tomatoes keep well in the fridge in an airtight container (try a large mason jar) for a week, or in the freezer in a sturdy plastic bag for 2 to 3 months.

# "Baked" Sweet Potatoes

If you love an oven-baked potato but don't love the wait—and try to avoid the quicker microwave method—this is a nice compromise. In just 18 minutes you'll have a perfectly done potato that you can slice and stuff with your favorite filling. Try it with the Chili-Style Kidney Beans on page 27.

**2 cups (470 ml) water**

**2 medium sweet potatoes**

Add the water to the pressure cooker. Insert a rack in the pressure cooker that will keep the potatoes well above the water. Put the potatoes on the rack. Cover and bring to pressure. Cook at high pressure for 18 minutes. Allow for a natural release. Remove the lid and pierce the potatoes with a fork to check for doneness. If not cooked through, bring back to pressure for 3 to 5 minutes and use a quick release.

Yield: 2 servings

# Mashed Peas and Potatoes

A colorful, quick mash, these bright green peas, a legume, pack a whopping 8 grams of protein. That means you can have this mashed potato dish as an entrée—guilt-free!

Salt

2 pounds (908 g) butter cream potatoes (or other small, new potatoes)

8 ounces (228 g) English peas, shelled

½ cup (120 ml) almond milk

2 tablespoons (28 g) vegan butter

¼ teaspoon thyme leaves

¼ teaspoon whole rosemary

Place a trivet in the pressure cooker, place a steamer basket on top of the trivet, and add enough water to come up to, but not in, the basket. Add a pinch of salt. Bring the water to a boil.

Scrub the potatoes (leave the skin on) and rinse the English peas. Place the potatoes in the steamer basket. Pour the peas over the potatoes.

Cover and bring to pressure. Cook at high pressure for 6 minutes. Use a quick release.

Uncover the pressure cooker and gently remove the steamer basket with kitchen tongs. Pour any remaining water out of the pressure cooker. Transfer the potatoes and peas back into the pressure cooker (alternatively, you can use a large bowl). Add the almond milk and butter. Mash with a potato masher to make this nice and chunky. Crumble the thyme leaves and whole rosemary with a mortar and pestle or by rubbing between your fingers and thumbs and sprinkle over the potatoes and peas and stir. Add salt to taste.

Yield: 4 servings

# Savory Root Vegetable Mash

## I'm partial to root vegetables in the pressure cooker because they

are so good for you and so delicious, but they often require a longer cook time, whether boiling or roasting. You can use any root vegetable that you like in this recipe.

4 carrots, cut into 2-inch (5 cm) pieces

5 or 6 whole baby turnips

2 cups (220 g) halved fingerling potatoes

2 cloves garlic, peeled but whole

1/2 teaspoon dried herbes de Provence

1/4 cup (60 ml) unsweetened almond milk

1/4 teaspoon sea salt (optional)

Freshly ground black pepper

Place a trivet in the pressure cooker, place a steamer basket on top of the trivet, and add enough water to come up to, but not in, the basket. Bring the water to a boil. Place the carrots, turnips, potatoes, and garlic in the steamer basket.

Cover and bring to pressure. Cook at high pressure for 6 minutes. Use a quick release.

Remove the lid, carefully remove the steamer basket with tongs, and transfer the vegetables to a large bowl. Add the herbes de Provence, almond milk, salt, and pepper to taste and mash with a hand masher. Serve immediately.

Yield: 6 servings

## Recipe Note

When making mashed potatoes and other root vegetables:

• You can always substitute plant milk for coconut oil for creaminess.

• Use vegetable broth if you want a lower fat version.

• Stir in a little maple syrup for added sweetness.

• To add an umami element, stir in caramelized onions after mashing.

# Holiday Roast with Mashed Vegetables

Times are changing. You can now find vegan stuffed roasts in grocery stores during the holiday season! I have baked and slow cooked a few, but I find pressure cooking the best way to prepare these dense, precooked roasts; the outcome is a soft, succulent dish.

1 to 2 teaspoons extra-virgin olive oil

4 cloves garlic, minced

1 cup (160 g) diced yellow onion

2 cups (260 g) diced carrot

2 cups (220 g) diced potato

1 teaspoon sea salt

1 vegan stuffed roast (1 pound, or 454 g), thawed

3/4 to 1 cup (180 to 235 ml) vegetable broth

1 tablespoon (15 ml) almond milk

1/4 teaspoon ground black pepper

1 teaspoon vegan butter (optional)

In an uncovered pressure cooker, heat the oil on medium-high. Add the garlic and onion and sauté for 1 minute. Add the carrots, potatoes, and salt. Mix well. Place the thawed roast on top of the vegetables and pour the vegetable broth over the roast.

Cover and bring to pressure. Cook at low pressure for 8 minutes. Use a quick release.

Remove the lid, remove the roast, and set aside.

Add the almond milk, black pepper, and vegan butter to the vegetables in the pressure cooker and mash with a potato masher. Slice the roast and serve with the mashed vegetables.

Yield: 4 servings

## Recipe Note

If you're using a multifunction electric pressure cooker, you can also use the slow-cooking function for 1 hour.

# Vegan "Loose Meat" Sandwiches

## Not a sloppy Joe and not quite a Maid-Rite, this is a vegan version

of a loose meat sandwich that is oh so simple and tasty! This filling is terrific served on a toasted bun with yellow mustard and onions. I have also used it for hard-shell tacos.

2 tablespoons (28 g)
  vegan butter

½ cup (80 g) diced onion

1 cup (70 g) diced mushrooms

½ teaspoon cumin

½ teaspoon garlic powder

¼ teaspoon sea salt, or more
  as needed

¼ teaspoon liquid smoke

½ cup (120 ml) almond milk

1 cup (100 g) TVP

½ cup (120 ml) vegetable broth

½ teaspoon ground
  black pepper

4 hamburger buns, toasted

In an uncovered pressure cooker, heat the butter on medium-high. Add the onion and mushrooms and sauté for 3 minutes, until the onion softens. Add the seasonings and almond milk and bring to a light boil. Add the TVP and vegetable broth and stir well.

Cover and bring to pressure. Cook at high pressure for 3 minutes. Use a quick release.

Remove the lid, stir in the pepper, and add more salt, if needed. Spoon onto the hamburger buns.

Yield: 4 sandwiches

# Pulled Jackfruit Sandwiches

Jackfruit is, well, a fruit. Its flesh is very meaty and, when cooked, it shreds, so it's become a darling among vegans who want to mimic shredded meat recipes.

1 teaspoon extra-virgin olive oil

¼ cup (40 g) finely diced onion

1 tablespoon (8 g) minced garlic

1 can (17 ounces, or 476 g) jackfruit, packed in water, rinsed and drained

½ teaspoon cayenne pepper

½ teaspoon yellow mustard seeds

½ teaspoon ground black pepper

½ teaspoon salt, or to taste

3 tablespoons (48 g) tomato paste

1 teaspoon apple cider vinegar

1 teaspoon vegan Worcestershire sauce

1 tablespoon (15 ml) maple, date, or brown rice syrup

½ to ¾ cup (120 to 180 ml) water

4 buns, toasted

In an uncovered pressure cooker heat the oil on medium-high. Add the onion and garlic and sauté for 3 minutes, until the onion is soft. Add the jackfruit, seasonings, tomato paste, vinegar, Worcestershire, and syrup and stir to combine. Add enough of the water to cover the jackfruit and mix well.

Cover and bring to pressure. Cook at high pressure for 3 minutes. Allow for a natural release.

Remove the lid and stir the jackfruit and sauce well. Use a fork to pull the jackfruit into shreds. This should be very easy to do. Serve on the toasted buns.

Yield: 4 servings

## Recipe Notes

- Canned jackfruit is often packed in syrup or sugar water and you do not want this! Look for the type that's packed in water or brine. Both varieties are most commonly found at Asian markets, but if you don't have one, try an online store.

- Remember, traditional Worcestershire contains anchovies—not vegan—so you'll want a vegan brand.

# Jackfruit and Sweet Potato Enchiladas

Enchiladas are often associated with meat and cheese. Here jack-fruit adds the meaty texture and mashed sweet potatoes lend a cheesy consistency, along with a little vegan cheese topping.

## FOR JACKFRUIT FILLING:

1 teaspoon extra-virgin olive oil

4 cloves garlic, finely diced

¼ cup (40 g) diced onion

¾ cup (83 g) diced sweet potato

1 can (17 ounces, or 476 g) jackfruit, packed in water, rinsed and drained

1 teaspoon ground cumin

2 teaspoons taco seasoning

1 teaspoon chili powder

¼ teaspoon salt

½ to 1 cup (120 to 235 ml) vegetable broth

## FOR ENCHILADAS:

1 can (12 ounces, or 336 g) red enchilada sauce

10 to 12 (6-inch, or 15 cm) corn tortillas

1 can (4 ounces, or 112 g) diced green chiles

1 can (2.25 ounces, 63 g) sliced black olives, drained

1 cup (120 g) shredded vegan cheddar cheese, to cover the enchiladas

Preheat the oven to 350°F (180°C, or gas mark 4). Grease a 13 x 7-inch (33 x 18 cm) baking dish.

**To make the jackfruit filling:** In an uncovered pressure cooker, heat the oil on medium-high. Add the garlic and onion and sauté for 3 minutes, until the onion is soft. Add the sweet potatoes and sauté for another minute or two. Add the jackfruit, cumin, taco seasoning, chili powder, salt, and enough vegetable broth to cover the potatoes and jackfruit. Stir well.

Cover and bring to pressure. Cook at high pressure for 3 minutes. Allow for a natural release.

Remove the lid, stir well, and use your spoon, or a fork, to shred the jackfruit. Set aside.

**To make the enchiladas:** In a shallow saucepan, heat the enchilada sauce over medium-low heat. Take each tortilla, one by one, and place into the saucepan to coat. Let each tortilla sit in the warm sauce for 20 to 30 seconds (turning once or twice to coat completely). Remove to a plate.

Once all tortillas are done, remove the sauce from heat and set aside. Take 1 tablespoon (15 g) filling and spread in the middle of the tortilla. Add some green chiles and black olive slices (about ½ teaspoon each). Fold or roll the tortilla and place in the prepared baking dish, seam-side down. Repeat with remaining tortillas, then pour the remaining sauce over them in the pan. Sprinkle with the cheese and the remaining olives and green chiles. Bake until heated through and bubbling, 20 to 25 minutes.

Yield: 10 to 12 enchiladas

# Tempeh Tacos or Tostadas

In this healthy twist on traditional Mexican fare, tempeh—a soy–based powerhouse packed with fiber, calcium, iron, vitamin B-6, and over 60 percent of USDA daily protein recommendations—offers a meaty texture that is 100 percent plant-based.

### FOR TEMPEH FILLING:

1 package (8 ounces, or 224 g) package tempeh

2 cups (470 ml) vegetable broth, divided

2 cloves garlic, minced

½ cup (80 g) diced red onion

¼ cup (30 g) finely diced celery

2 cups (140 g) diced cremini mushrooms

1 seeded and diced fresh jalapeño

½ cup (130 g) mild salsa

1 to 2 teaspoons chili powder

Juice of ½ lime

½ teaspoon salt

### FOR SPINACH:

1 teaspoon extra-virgin olive oil

2 cloves garlic, minced

8 cups (480 g) loosely packed baby spinach

Pinch of salt

Juice of ½ lime

6 taco shells or corn tortillas, baked or fried in oil until crispy

½ cup (120 g) vegan sour cream

1 lime, cut into 6 wedges

**To make the tempeh:** Cut tempeh into 4 equal pieces. Add to an uncovered pressure cooker with 1 cup (235 ml) of the vegetable broth. Cover and bring to pressure. As soon as pressure is achieved use a quick release.

Remove the lid and return to medium-high heat. Crumble the tempeh into a "ground meat" consistency with a spoon. Add the garlic, onion, celery, mushrooms, jalapeño, and salsa. Everything will be boiling. Add the chili powder and remaining 1 cup (235 ml) vegetable broth. Stir well.

Cover and return to pressure. Cook at high pressure for 3 minutes. Allow for a natural release. Remove the lid, add the lime juice and salt, and simmer on low to cook off the extra liquid.

**To make the spinach:** Heat the olive oil in a skillet over medium-high heat. Add the garlic and spinach and sauté for 30 seconds, tossing with tongs to prevent sticking. Add the salt and lime juice, toss, and remove from the heat.

Place a layer of spinach on each of the tacos shells or corn tortillas for tostadas. Add the tempeh and a dollop of sour cream and serve with a wedge of lime.

Yield: 6 servings

## Recipe Note

Follow the first step in this recipe *anytime* you are using tempeh! It's a super quick way to steam it, which softens it and prepares it to absorb your marinade of choice.

# Italian Soybean Balls
# and Tomato Sauce

Thanks to a food processor and the pressure cooker, this meal comes together quickly. While the soybean balls are cooking, heat up water in a pan and make your favorite pasta. You'll be enjoying a soybean ball and tomato sauce pasta dish in less than 30 minutes!

**FOR SOYBEAN BALLS:**

1 cup (200 g) dried black soybeans, soaked for 12 hours or overnight

2 to 3 cups (470 to 705 ml) water plus 6 tablespoons (90 ml) warm water, divided

1 tablespoon (15 ml) vegetable oil

½ cup (50 g) TVP

½ cup (120 ml) vegetable broth, warm

2 tablespoons (14 g) ground flaxseed

2 tablespoons (16 g) black sesame seeds

2 tablespoons (14 g) Italian herb bread crumbs

1 teaspoon salt

2 tablespoons (14 g) nutritional yeast

2 tablespoons (14 g) Italian seasoning

½ teaspoon red pepper flakes

½ teaspoon black pepper

**To make the soybean balls:** Rinse and drain the soaked black soybeans. Add to a pressure cooker with the 2 to 3 cups (470 to 705 ml) water, enough to cover the beans by 2 inches (5 cm), and the oil. Cover and bring to pressure. Cook at high pressure for 20 to 22 minutes—opt for the lower cooking time here to give the beans a bit of a "crunch" as they will continue cooking when the soybean balls are cooked with the sauce. Allow for a natural release; if after 10 minutes the pressure has still not come down fully, manually release.

Meanwhile, soak the TVP in the warm vegetable broth in a bowl for 10 minutes.

Prepare the flax egg by whisking the ground flaxseed in the remaining 6 tablespoons (90 ml) warm water and let sit for 10 minutes.

Pulse the black soybeans, TVP, flax egg, sesame seeds, bread crumbs, salt, nutritional yeast, Italian seasoning, red pepper flakes, and black pepper in a food processor for 15 seconds, long enough to mix well but avoid liquefying or making too creamy.

Make soybean balls by scooping out 2 to 3 tablespoons (28 to 42 g) and rolling in your hands. You should get about 36 balls. Set the soybean balls aside.

## FOR SAUCE:

1 tablespoon (15 ml) vegetable oil

3 cloves garlic, minced

1 cup (160 g) diced red onion

½ cup (75 g) diced green bell pepper

½ cup (75 g) diced red bell pepper

1 cup (130 g) diced carrot

1 can (15 ounces, or 425 g) tomato sauce

1½ cup (354 ml) vegetable broth

2 tablespoons (14 g) Italian seasoning

½ teaspoon black pepper

Cooked pasta of choice

**To make the sauce:** In an uncovered pressure cooker heat the oil on medium-high. Add the garlic, onion, peppers, and carrots and sauté, stirring frequently, for 5 minutes. If necessary, add water to avoid sticking. Stir in the tomato sauce, broth, Italian seasoning, and black pepper. Gingerly place the soybean balls in the sauce.

Cover and bring to pressure. Cook at low pressure for 2 minutes. Use a quick release.

Remove the lid. Spoon over the cooked pasta.

Yield: 4 servings; 36 soybean balls

## Recipe Notes

- I make soybean balls all the time. Sometimes they come out as perfect, round balls and sometimes they come apart a bit. When that happens I just stir vigorously and turn it into soy-meat sauce—we love it that way, too!

- You can make the black beans 2 or 3 days in advance and store in an airtight container in the refrigerator.

- If you want to skip the oil in the sauce, substitute ¼ cup (60 ml) water or vegetable broth.

- If you don't have Italian herb bread crumbs, substitute whatever type you have (or make your own!).

# Fiesta Soy Curl and Rice Casserole

## Soy curls are a great substitute for traditional chicken dishes.

Made from the whole soybean, they are packed with protein and extremely versatile. A loose casserole, this is best served in a bowl. For a fun treat, serve it on top of blue or yellow corn tortilla chips and enjoy a hearty plate of nachos for lunch or dinner.

3 cups (300 g) soy curls

4 cups (940 ml) vegetable broth, warm, divided

1 teaspoon extra-virgin olive oil

2 cloves garlic, minced

½ cup (80 g) diced yellow onion

2 tablespoons (16 g) vegan chicken-flavored seasoning

1 tablespoon (8 g) taco seasoning

1 cup (190 g) long-grain white rice

1 can (15.25-ounce, or 427 g) corn, drained

1 can (28 ounces, or 784 g) diced tomatoes with green chiles

1 can (8 ounces, or 224 g) tomato sauce

½ to 1 teaspoon sea salt

1½ cups (180 g) shredded vegan cheese, divided

1 cup (70 g) crumbled corn tortilla chips

Freshly ground black pepper

Preheat the oven to 375°F (190°C, or gas mark 5). Grease a 13 x 7-inch (33 x 18 cm) casserole dish.

Soak the soy curls in 3 cups (705 ml) of the warm vegetable broth in a bowl for 15 minutes. Drain the soy curls and set aside.

In an uncovered pressure cooker, heat the olive oil on medium-high. Add the garlic and onion and sauté for 3 minutes, until the onion is soft. Add the drained soy curls, chicken-flavored seasoning, and taco seasoning and sauté for 3 to 5 minutes. Note: Soy curls, much like tofu, need time to absorb the flavors. Add water or vegetable broth if they begin to stick to the pan. Add the rice, corn, tomatoes and chiles, tomato sauce, and remaining 1 cup (235 ml) vegetable broth and mix well.

Cover and bring to pressure. Cook at high pressure for 4 minutes. Use a quick release.

Remove the lid. Taste and add salt as needed. Stir in 1 cup (120 g) of the shredded vegan cheese. Transfer to the prepared casserole dish.

In a small bow, mix the remaining ½ cup (60 g) shredded vegan cheese with the crumbled tortilla chips. Sprinkle over the casserole.

Bake for 10 minutes, or until the cheese is melted. Serve with freshly ground black pepper.

Yield: 8 to 10 servings

# Refried Beans

These beans are great as a side dish when making a full Mexican
dinner but you can also use them as the filling for tacos or on top of vegan nachos as an entrée.
I love to spread them on a whole-wheat tortilla with chopped lettuce, shredded vegan cheddar
cheese, and a dollop of sour cream for a Mexican-style wrap sandwich.

1 cup (200 g) dried pinto
   beans, soaked for 12 hours
   or overnight

1 tablespoon (15 ml) extra-
   virgin olive oil

1/2 cup (80 g) diced
   yellow onion

4 cloves garlic, minced

1 or 2 seeded and diced fresh
   jalapeños

2 to 3 cups (470 to 705 ml)
   water or vegetable broth

1 teaspoon chili powder

1/2 teaspoon cumin

1/4 teaspoon cayenne pepper

1/2 to 1 teaspoon salt

Rinse and drain the beans.

In an uncovered pressure cooker, heat the oil on
medium-high. Add the onion, garlic, and jalapeño and
sauté for 3 minutes, until the onion is soft. Add the pinto
beans and enough water or vegetable broth to cover the
beans plus another 1 inch (2.5 cm) of liquid. Add the chili
powder, cumin, and cayenne pepper. Stir to combine.

Cover and bring to pressure. Cook for 6 minutes at
high pressure. Allow for a natural release.

Remove the lid, drain the beans (reserve the liquid
in a measure cup) and return the beans to the pressure
cooker. Add salt to taste. Begin mashing the beans with
a hand masher. For a creamier refried beans, add some
of the cooking liquid as needed.

Yield: 4 to 6 servings

# White Beans and Rice

A vegan twist on traditional red beans and rice with sausage, this dish uses white beans, brown rice, and vegan pepperoni. This is a meal helper because you can make the beans, rice, and even homemade pepperoni (page 149) anytime and bring them together for this meal.

1 cup (200 g) dried navy beans, soaked for 12 hours or overnight

1 teaspoon extra-virgin olive oil

½ cup (80 g) diced sweet onion

2 cloves garlic, minced

½ teaspoon cayenne pepper

1 bay leaf

2 to 3 cups (470 to 705 ml) vegetable broth

1½ cups (262 g) cubed vegan pepperoni sausage, homemade (page 149) or store-bought

½ teaspoon salt, or to taste

3 cups (480 g) cooked brown rice, for serving

Rinse and drain the beans.

In an uncovered pressure cooker, heat the oil on medium-high. Add the onion and garlic and sauté for 2 to 3 minutes, until softened. Add the cayenne pepper, bay leaf, and beans. Stir in the vegetable broth to cover, plus another 1 inch (2.5 cm) of liquid. Stir to combine.

Cover and bring to pressure. Cook at high pressure for 6 to 8 minutes. Allow for a natural release.

Remove the lid. Stir in the pepperoni sausage and let simmer, uncovered, for a few minutes to heat the sausage through. Taste and season with salt, if needed. Serve over the brown rice.

Yield: 4 to 6 servings

# Mediterranean Beans with Greens

This dish epitomizes the Mediterranean diet—low in saturated
fats, high in fiber and other nutrients. Plus, it pleases vegans and omnivores alike! I created a stove
top version of this recipe for my book *Vegan for Her*; cooking the beans, tomatoes, and olives
together in the pressure cooker intensifies the flavor immensely.

1 cup (200 g) dried navy or
cannellini beans, soaked for
12 hours or overnight

2 cups (470 ml) vegetable broth

2 cans (14.5 ounces, or 406 g)
cans diced tomatoes with basil,
garlic, and oregano

½ cup (50 g) sliced green olives,
plus extra for garnish

1 teaspoon extra-virgin olive oil

4 cloves garlic, finely diced

8 cups (140 g) loosely packed
arugula (about 5 ounces,
or 140 g)

½ cup (120 ml) freshly squeezed
lemon juice, divided

Pinch of salt

2 cups (320 g) cooked pearl
barley (see page 41)

Rinse and drain the beans.

Add the beans, broth, diced tomatoes, and olives to
the pressure cooker. Cover and bring to pressure. Cook
at high pressure for 6 to 8 minutes. Allow for a natural
release.

While the beans are cooking, heat the olive oil in a
skillet over medium-high heat. Add the garlic and sauté
until soft but not brown, 1 to 2 minutes. Add the arugula
and ¼ cup (60 ml) of the lemon juice to the skillet and,
using tongs, turn the arugula frequently for 30 seconds.
It will wilt quickly, which is what you want, but remove
from the heat before turning brown. Set aside.

Remove the lid from the pressure cooker and stir in
the remaining ¼ cup (60 ml) lemon juice. Taste. The
olives and tomatoes should be sufficient, but add salt,
if desired.

To serve, begin with a plate of cooked pearl barley,
add the arugula, and then top with the beans and tomatoes. Add a few olive slices for garnish.

Yield: 4 servings

## Recipe Note

To keep this recipe simple, I buy diced tomatoes
seasoned with basil, garlic, and oregano. If you opt
for a can of plain diced tomatoes, consider adding
basil, garlic, and oregano for extra flavor.

# Basic Seitan

## Seitan, also known as "wheat meat," can take on a variety of flavors

simply by changing up the spices and seasoning. Follow this recipe, or swap out the cumin and Italian seasoning for 1 ½ teaspoons of the spices of your choice and you change the flavor but not the texture. This makes a great plant-based dinner, as it is familiar in both taste and texture to meat-based dishes. Chickpea flour is also labeled as garbanzo bean, gram, or besan flour at Asian grocers.

**FOR SEITAN:**

1½ cups (180 g) vital wheat gluten

¼ cup (30 g) chickpea flour

2 tablespoons (14 g) nutritional yeast

½ teaspoon garlic powder

½ teaspoon ground black pepper

½ teaspoon ground ginger

½ teaspoon ground cinnamon

½ teaspoon ground cumin

1 cup (235 ml) vegetable broth

1 teaspoon avocado oil

1 teaspoon blackstrap molasses

2 tablespoons (30 ml) Bragg Liquid Aminos or soy sauce

**FOR BROTH:**

3 cups (705 ml) water

3 cups (705 ml) vegetable broth

¼ cup (60 ml) low-sodium soy sauce

**To make the seitan:** Combine the gluten, chickpea flour, nutritional yeast, and seasonings in a medium bowl or a stand mixer. In a separate bowl, whisk together the broth, oil, molasses, and liquid aminos. Add the wet ingredients to the dry ingredients and stir until well combined.

Knead for 5 minutes, either by hand or using the dough hook of the stand mixer.

Roll the dough into one long log and slice into 6 cutlets. Set aside.

**To make the broth:** In an uncovered pressure cooker add the broth ingredients and bring to a boil.

Add the cutlets, cover, and bring to pressure. Cook at low pressure for 30 minutes. Remove from the heat and allow for a natural release.

Remove the cutlets from the broth to cool before handling or serving.

Yield: 6 seitan cutlets; 8 to 10 servings

## Recipe Note

Store leftover cutlets in the cooking broth in an airtight container in the refrigerator or in a sturdy bag in the freezer.

# Seitan-Stuffed Acorn Squash

When I make homemade seitan (page 146), I often crumble a portion and store it, in broth, in the freezer. It's a great substitute for recipes calling for ground meat. You can also find crumbled meat alternatives in the freezer section of many grocery stores.

1 acorn squash

Pinch of sea salt

1 teaspoon extra-virgin olive oil

¼ cup (40 g) chopped onion

¼ cup (30 g) chopped celery

1 cup (110 g) crumbled seitan

1 cup (70 g) diced shiitake mushrooms

½ teaspoon dried sage

¼ teaspoon dried thyme

¼ teaspoon ground black pepper

1 teaspoon Sriracha or your favorite hot sauce

Cut the squash in half and scoop out the seeds. Cut or scoop out enough squash flesh to make room for ½ cup (55 g) of the seitan filling in each cavity—you'll end up with about ¼ cup (40 g) squash flesh: chop and set aside. Sprinkle a little salt over the squash halves and set aside.

In a skillet, heat the olive oil over medium-high heat. Add the onion and celery and sauté until the onion is translucent, 2 to 3 minutes. Add the chopped squash, seitan, mushrooms, sage, thyme, pepper, and Sriracha and stir to combine. Sauté for about 5 minutes, until the seitan is lightly browned. Spoon the sautéed seitan mixture into the 2 squash halves.

Place a trivet in the pressure cooker, place a steamer basket on top of the trivet, and add enough water to come up to, but not in, the basket. Bring the water to a boil. Place the squash in the steamer basket. If the squash halves do not fit in the basket, turn the basket upside down for a flat surface. Place foil loosely over the top of the squash.

Cover and bring to pressure. Cook at pressure for 10 minutes. Use a quick release.

Remove the pressure cooker lid, remove the foil, and let the squash sit for 3 to 5 minutes in the uncovered pressure cooker. Remove the squash from the pressure cooker with tongs (handle gently) and serve.

Yield: 2 servings

# Vegan "Pepperoni" Sausage

This seitan is an alternative to a favorite pizza topping and can be made quickly and easily in the pressure cooker. You can cut thicker slices and serve as a sausage patty with breakfast, dice up and serve in cooked beans, or even serve on crackers for an appetizer. In this recipe I suggest that you make four smaller sausages and one larger one so that you can have larger seitan cutlets for breakfast patties and smaller sausages for pepperoni slices.

**FOR COOKING BROTH:**

3 cups (705 ml) water

3 cups (705 ml) vegetable broth

¼ cup (60 ml) low-sodium soy sauce

**FOR SEITAN:**

1½ cups (180 g) vital wheat gluten

¼ cup (30 g) chickpea flour

2 tablespoons (14 g) nutritional yeast

½ teaspoon allspice

½ teaspoon paprika

½ teaspoon anise seed

½ teaspoon fennel seed, crumbled

½ teaspoon red pepper flakes

½ teaspoon garlic powder

½ teaspoon ground black pepper

1 cup (235 ml) vegetable broth, plus more as needed

1 teaspoon extra-virgin olive oil

2 tablespoons (30 ml) soy sauce

½ teaspoon vegan Worcestershire sauce

½ teaspoon liquid smoke

**To make the broth:** In an uncovered pressure cooker, add the broth ingredients and bring to a boil.

**To make the seitan:** Combine the gluten, chickpea flour, nutritional yeast, and seasonings in the bowl of a stand mixer fitted with the dough hook attachment. In a separate bowl, whisk together the broth, oil, liquid smoke, Worcestershire sauce, and liquid aminos. Add the wet ingredients to the dry ingredients and stir until well combined. Knead with the dough hook for 5 minutes.

Divided the dough in half. From one half, roll 4 small sausages and wrap individually in cheesecloth, tying the ends with string. Take the remaining half and roll into a larger sausage and wrap in cheesecloth, tying the ends with string.

Place in the boiling cooking broth, cover, and bring to pressure. Cook at pressure for 30 minutes. Allow for a natural release.

Remove the sausages from the broth to cool before handling or serving.

Yield: 8 to 10 servings

## Recipe Note

If you don't have allspice, substitute a mixture of ground nutmeg, cinnamon, and cloves equal to ½ teaspoon.

# CHAPTER SIX

# Sauces and Dips

**Pressure cooking is a great way to prepare beans and vegetables** in advance and turn them into amazing additions to a meal. I love thawing beans and tossing them into the food processor for a quick, wholesome dip or to use in gravy.

# Marinara Sauce

## This is a very quick sauce that

stores well in an airtight container in the refrigerator or in the freezer. You can use it with pasta, over cooked grains, or even add to soups to thicken and boost flavor.

|||||||||||||||||||||||||||||||||||||||||||||||||||||

1 teaspoon extra-virgin olive oil

4 to 6 cloves garlic, minced

1 cup (160 g) diced onion

1 teaspoon dried basil

1 teaspoon dried oregano

1 teaspoon dried parsley

1 teaspoon dried thyme

1/2 teaspoon red pepper flakes

1/4 teaspoon black pepper

1 can (28 ounces, or 784 g) crushed tomatoes

1/2 cup (120 ml) vegetable broth

1/2 teaspoon sea salt

1/2 teaspoon sugar (optional)

In an uncovered pressure cooker, heat the oil on medium-high. Add the garlic and onion and sauté for 3 minutes, until the onion is soft. Add the seasonings, tomatoes, and broth. Stir to combine.

Cover and bring to pressure. Cook at low pressure for 5 minutes. Allow for a natural release.

Remove the lid, taste, and add salt and sugar as desired.

Yield: 4 to 6 servings

# Lentil Pâté

## While many people think of

pâté as decidedly not vegan, there are many vegetable versions on the market and in restaurants. The lentils in this pâté add a rich color and a creamy texture. Serve with raw vegetables, pita chips, or even as a sandwich spread.

|||||||||||||||||||||||||||||||||||||||||||||||||||||

1 cup (200 g) dried lentils

2 cups (470 ml) water or vegetable broth

2 cloves garlic, minced

1 tablespoon (15 ml) lime juice

1 teaspoon sesame seeds

1/2 teaspoon sesame or extra-virgin olive oil

Add the lentils and water to the pressure cooker. Cover and bring to pressure. Cook at high pressure for 8 to 10 minutes. Allow for a natural release.

Drain the lentils, then add the lentils, lime juice, sesame seeds, and oil to a food processor. Pulse, scraping down the sides as needed, to a thick, pâté consistency.

Yield: 4 to 6 servings

# Ginger-Cinnamon White Bean Gravy

This protein-packed gravy is perfect to serve over mashed potatoes (page 124) and seitan (page 146). White beans, puréed, replace the need for any type of dairy. I include this recipe in all of my holiday cooking classes because it's a student favorite.

IIIIIIIIIIIIIIIIIIIIIIIIIIIIIIIIIIIIIIIIIIIIIIIIIIIIIIIIIIIIIIIIIIIIIIIIIIIIIIIIIIIIIIIIIIIIIIIIIIIIII

1 cup (200 g) dried navy beans, soaked for 12 hours or overnight

1 teaspoon olive oil

3 cloves garlic, coarsely chopped

4 cups (940 ml) water

1 bay leaf

Juice of 1 lemon (about 2 tablespoons, or 30 ml)

4 tablespoons (56 g) vegan butter

½ cup (80 g) chopped yellow onion

⅛ teaspoon ground ginger

⅛ teaspoon ground cinnamon

⅛ teaspoon freshly ground black pepper

1 cup (235 ml) low-sodium vegetable broth

¼ cup (60 ml) low-sodium soy sauce

2 tablespoons (14 g) nutritional yeast (flakes or powder)

Rinse and drain the beans.

In an uncovered pressure cooker, heat the oil on medium. Add the beans, garlic, water, and bay leaf. Cover and bring to pressure. Cook at high pressure for 6 to 8 minutes. Allow for a natural release.

Remove the lid and stir in the lemon juice. Taste for doneness. If the beans are not fully cooked, simmer on low, uncovered. Set aside.

Heat the butter in a large saucepan over medium-high heat. Once the butter is melted, add the onion and sauté until translucent, 2 to 3 minutes. Add the ground ginger, cinnamon, and pepper and stir well. Stir in the broth and soy sauce. Bring to a boil. Reduce the heat and add 1½ cups (1.3 kg) of the cooked beans, using a slotted spoon. Save the remaining beans for a salad or use in the White Bean Dip (page 160).

Blend the gravy using either an immersion blender in the saucepan or transfer to a blender and pulse for 20 to 30 seconds. If using a blender, return the gravy back to the saucepan once blended.

Stir in the nutritional yeast, cover the saucepan, and cook over medium heat for 5 minutes, stirring occasionally, until slightly thickened.

Serve warm, over mashed potatoes (page 124) or root vegetables (page 129) or with a holiday roast (page 130). Leftover gravy is fantastic over seitan cutlets (page 146) or biscuits.

Yield: 3 to 4 cups (780 to 1040 g)

# Chickpea Hummus

## The first time I made traditional hummus in the pressure cooker

I realized there was no need to buy it from a store again. In this recipe, I add key ingredients such as onion and garlic into the cooking process itself (rather than after) and the flavors—and creamy texture—cannot be beat. I predict this will become a favorite recipe of yours too!

||||||||||||||||||||||||||||||||||||||||||||||||||||||||||||||||||||||||||||||||||||||||||||||||||||

1 cup (200 g) dried chickpeas, soaked for 12 hours or overnight

1 tablespoon (15 ml) sesame oil

½ cup (80 g) diced yellow onion

4 or 5 cloves garlic, minced

½ to 1 teaspoon sea salt

¼ cup (60 g) tahini

¼ cup (60 ml) lemon juice

Rinse and drain the chickpeas.

In an uncovered pressure cooker, heat the oil on medium-high. Add the onion and garlic and sauté for 3 minutes, until the onion is translucent. Add the chickpeas and enough water to cover, plus another 1 inch (2.5 cm).

Cover and bring to pressure. Cook at high pressure for 13 to 15 minutes. Allow for a natural release.

Remove the lid and stir in the salt. Drain the chickpeas, reserving the cooking broth.

Add the chickpeas, tahini, and lemon juice to a food processor. Pulse to a creamy texture, adding the cooking broth as needed if the mixture is too dry. Taste and add extra salt if needed.

Yield: 4 to 6 servings

# Pesto-Style Bean Dip

**Traditional pesto is a sauce with garlic, basil, and pine nuts, most** often blended with cheese and olive oil. There are lots of variations, and in this recipe, I went with the basic flavors and turned it into a dip that works easily in sandwiches or on salads for an entrée. Mortgage Lifters beans are a really creamy heirloom bean. If you can't find them, use butter or lima beans.

1 cup (200 g) dried Mortgage Lifter beans, soaked overnight

4 cups (940 ml) water

2 bay leaves

1 tablespoon (5 g) dried oregano

2 cloves garlic, minced

1 cup (40 g) tightly packed fresh basil leaves, chopped coarsely

½ cup (66 g) Brazil nuts, coarsely chopped

2 tablespoons (14 g) nutritional yeast

¼ cup (60 ml) lemon juice

½ teaspoon salt

¼ to ½ cup (60 to 118 ml) reserved bean broth (optional)

Rinse and drain the beans. Add beans, water, bay leaves, oregano, and garlic to the pressure cooker. Cover, heat on medium-high, and bring to pressure. Cook at high pressure for 18 to 20 minutes. Allow for a natural release.

Drain beans through a mesh strainer over a bowl to save the bean broth. Do not rinse the beans.

Transfer the beans to a food processor. Add remaining ingredients and pulse until a creamy consistency has been achieved. Use reserved bean broth if it requires more liquid.

Yield: Makes 3 cups (700 g)

# North-Meets-South Bean Dip

Here's a quick and easy legume dip, featuring northern and pinto beans, perfect as a spread for veggies or crackers, as the star of a veggie sandwich wrap, or as a topper to a very veggie salad.

½ cup (100 g) dry northern beans, soaked overnight

½ cup (100 g) pinto beans, soaked overnight

2 to 3 cloves garlic, peeled and chopped coarsely

3 cups (705 ml) water or vegetable broth

2 tablespoons (30 g) tahini

2 tablespoons (30 ml) fresh lemon juice

½ teaspoon dried chili pepper

¼ cup (4 g) coarsely chopped cilantro

¼ to ½ teaspoon sea salt

1 to 2 tablespoons (15 to 30 ml) water

Rinse and drain the beans. Add the beans and enough water to cover, plus another 1 inch (2.5 cm), to the pressure cooker. Cover and bring to pressure. Cook at high pressure for 6 minutes. Allow for a natural release.

Drain the beans. Add the beans and the remaining ingredients, except the remaining water, to the food processor. Pulse quickly so that you can cream the beans but leave a few chunks (add water, as needed).

Yield: Makes 3 cups (700 g)

157

# Dal Dip

Traditional Indian dal is a soup with red lentils. Keeping true to the spices but using less liquid, this super-healthy dip is perfect on Indian breads, such as naan or roti, as well as crackers and raw vegetables.

||||||||||||||||||||||||||||||||||||||||||||||||||||||||||||||||||||||||||||||||||||||||||||||||||

1 tablespoon (15 ml) sesame oil

2 cloves garlic, minced

1 cup (130 g) diced carrot

1-inch (2.5 cm) piece ginger root, minced or grated (about 2 teaspoons)

1/2 teaspoon cumin

1/2 teaspoon fennel seeds

1 cup (180 g) diced fresh tomato

1 cup (200 g) dried red lentils

2 1/4 cups (530 ml) water

2 tablespoons (30 ml) lemon juice

In an uncovered pressure cooker, heat the oil on medium-high. Add the garlic, carrot, and ginger root and sauté for 2 minutes. Add the cumin, fennel seeds, tomato, lentils, and water. Stir to combine.

Cover and bring to pressure. Cook at high pressure for 5 minutes. Allow for a natural release.

Remove the lid. Stir in the lemon juice. Transfer to a food processor or high-speed blender and pulse quickly. This should not take more than 10 seconds. Refrigerate for at least 2 hours but overnight is best. Serve cold.

Yield: 1 1/2 to 2 cups

# Spicy Red Bean Hummus

**Although many of us know the** traditional hummus of chickpeas, tahini, and lemon juice, there are all kinds of beans and flavor profiles to play with. This one is perfect for topping crackers, dipping raw vegetables, or on a sandwich.

1 cup (200 g) dried kidney beans, soaked for 12 hours or overnight

1 seeded and diced fresh jalapeño

3 cloves garlic, minced

1 tablespoon (15 ml) lime juice

1 teaspoon taco seasoning

½ teaspoon cayenne pepper

1 tablespoon (15 ml) extra-virgin olive oil

½ teaspoon sea salt

Rinse and drain the beans.

Add the beans and enough water to cover, plus another 1 inch 2.5 cm), to the pressure cooker. Cover and bring to pressure. Cook at high pressure for 5 to 8 minutes. Allow for a natural release.

Drain the beans. Add the beans, jalapeño, garlic, lime juice, seasonings, oil, and salt to a food processor. Pulse to a creamy consistency.

Yield: 4 to 6 servings

# White Bean Dip

**My friend and** *Vegan for Her* coauthor Ginny Messina is a big fan of simple, wholesome snacks with big flavor. This dip is inspired by her casual mention of "just puree white beans with sun-dried tomatoes."

1 cup (200 g) dried white beans, soaked for 12 hours or overnight

2 to 3 cups (470 to 705 ml) water or vegetable broth

½ cup (55 g) oil-packed sun-dried tomatoes, thinly sliced

Rinse and drain the beans.

Add the beans and enough of the water or broth to cover, plus another 1 inch (2.5 cm), to the pressure cooker. Cover and bring to pressure. Cook at high pressure for 6 to 8 minutes. Allow for a natural release.

Drain the beans. Add the beans and sun-dried tomatoes, with oil, to a food processor. Pulse to a thick purée.

Yield: 4 to 6 servings

## Recipe Note

Modify this recipe by swapping out the fennel seeds and cumin with your favorite Indian spices, such as cardamom, cinnamon, coriander, garam masala, nutmeg, or saffron.

# CHAPTER SEVEN

# Sweet Treats

You might not think of a pressure cooker when it comes to dessert, but if you have a sweet tooth you can make most of these recipes in no time.

# Coconut-Gingered
# Black Bean Brownies

Black bean brownies are not a new concept, but it took a while for me to fall in love with them. I decided to experiment with subtle, less "sweet" flavors—and bring my love of using my pressure cooker for homemade beans into play. These brownies are not very sweet, so consider serving them with your favorite vegan ice cream.

1½ to 2 cups (300 to 400 g) dried black beans, soaked for 12 hours or overnight

6 tablespoons (90 ml) maple, date, or brown rice syrup, divided

1 (13.5-ounce, or 378 g) can organic light coconut milk

¾ cup (184 g) no-sugar-added applesauce

2 teaspoons pure vanilla extract

1 tablespoon (8 g) freshly grated ginger or 1 teaspoon ground

½ cup (60 g) cacao powder

½ cup (60 g) millet flour (or substitute oat, quinoa, or sorghum flour)

2 tablespoons (20 g) chunks dark chocolate, chopped from a bar

¼ cup (30 g) chopped walnuts

Preheat the oven to 350°F (180°C, or gas mark 4). Line a 9 x 9-inch (23 x 23 cm) baking dish with parchment paper.

Rinse and drain the beans. Add the beans, 2 tablespoons (30 ml) of the syrup, and coconut milk to the pressure cooker. Stir to combine. Cover and bring to pressure. Cook at high pressure for 12 minutes. Allow for a natural release.

Remove the lid. If beans are not done, simmer uncovered for 5 to 10 minutes, or until cooked through.

Pour the cooked beans into a food processor fitted with an S blade and pulse to chop up the beans. Add the applesauce, vanilla, ginger, and remaining 4 tablespoons (60 ml) syrup and blend until smooth. Add the cacao powder and flour, and blend until smooth, resembling a cake batter. Add half of the dark chocolate and half of the chopped walnuts to the food processor and quickly pulse (don't blend) so the pieces are mixed in but still chunky.

Pour the batter into the prepared baking dish. Sprinkle the remaining half of the chocolate and walnut pieces on top. Bake for 40 to 50 minutes, or until a toothpick inserted into the center comes out almost clean. These brownies are fudgy, so the toothpick will still have some moist crumbs clinging to it. If necessary, bake for 5 to 10 minutes longer.

Remove the brownies and the parchment paper from the baking dish and let cool on a rack for 20 minutes. Slice into squares and serve.

Yield: 12 brownies

# Fruit and Nut Rice Pudding

## Back in my vegetarian days, rice pudding was my hands-down

favorite dessert. On a trip to India I saved my appetite at every meal to enjoy it. Once
vegan, I found rice pudding recipes to be a bit lacking—until I tried it in the pressure cooker!

||||||||||||||||||||||||||||||||||||||||||||||||||||||||||||||||||||||||||||||||||||||||||||||||||||||||||||||||||||||||||||||||||||||

4 tablespoons (56 g) vegan butter

1 cup (190 g) Arborio rice

3 1/2 cups (822 ml) unsweetened
vanilla almond milk

2 to 3 tablespoons (30 to 45 ml)
maple, date, or brown rice
syrup

1 teaspoon pure vanilla extract

1/2 teaspoon pure almond extract

1/4 teaspoon ground cinnamon,
plus more for garnish

1/4 cup (35 g) golden raisins

1/4 cup (35 g) chopped dried
apricots

1/2 cup (55 g) slivered almonds

In an uncovered pressure cooker heat the vegan butter
on medium. Add the rice and stir to cover. Stir in the
almond milk.

Cover and bring to pressure. Cook at high pressure for
7 minutes. Use a quick release.

Remove the cover and stir in the syrup, extracts,
cinnamon, raisins, apricots, and almonds. Serve warm or
chilled with an extra sprinkle of ground cinnamon.

Yield: 6 servings

# Easy Applesauce

Every fall I pick up lots of apples and then think, "Uh-oh, now what do I do with them?" This applesauce is a speedy and delicious way to avoid wasting seasonal fruit. Stir it into cooked oatmeal, serve over vegan ice cream or, of course, enjoy it on it's own with a sprinkle of cinnamon.

|||||||||||||||||||||||||||||||||||||||||||||||||||||||||||||||||||||||||||||||||||||||||||||||||||||||||||||||||||||||

**4 cups (600 g) peeled, cored, and diced apple**

**2 teaspoons ground cinnamon**

**½ cup (120 ml) water**

**½ teaspoon sugar (optional)**

Add the apples, cinnamon, and water to the pressure cooker. Stir to combine. Cover and bring to pressure. Cook at high pressure for 3 minutes. Use a quick release. Remove the lid. Mash the apples with a potato masher and add sugar to taste.

Yield: 4 servings

## Recipe Note

The chunks of tender apples can be mashed to the consistency of your choice with a potato masher, or immersion blender—pour it into the food processor and purée it to make it baby-friendly!

# Quick Fruit Jam

My friend Justin Trollé is an elite triathlon coach and father of six.
I introduced him to pressure cooking. He introduced me to this jam—a necessity, he says, when making peanut butter and jelly for his large family.

4 cups (440 g) strawberries, raspberries, or blackberries

1 cup (235 ml) water

1 cup (200 g) sugar

3 teaspoons (14 g) pectin

1 teaspoon lemon or lime juice

Add the fruit and water to the pressure cooker. Cover and bring to pressure. Cook at low pressure for 10 minutes. Use a quick release.

Remove the lid and mash the fruit with a potato masher until the fruit is broken up. Add the sugar, pectin, and lemon juice. Simmer, uncovered, stirring every couple of minutes, until the jam is tacky on the spoon, 8 to 10 minutes.

Pour through a funnel or ladle the jam into jars. Let cool before sealing with an airtight lid.

Yield: 4 cups (440 g)

# Peachy Butter

## This very simple recipe makes a lightly sweet spread that is terrific

on fresh-baked sweet bread, such as banana bread or even on oats for breakfast. For dessert drizzle it over vegan ice cream. In addition to being simple and delicious, peaches are a good source of vitamin C.

3 cups (510 g) diced peaches

1 cup (235 ml) water

1 teaspoon ground cinnamon

1 teaspoon vegan butter

Add the peaches, water, and cinnamon to the pressure cooker. Cover and bring to pressure. Cook at high pressure for 3 minutes. Use a quick release method.

Remove the cover and mash the peaches with a potato masher. Add the vegan butter and simmer on low, uncovered, for 2 to 3 minutes to cook down any excess liquid; it should have a thick, jam-like consistency.

Yield: 2 cups (500 g)

## Recipe Note

Nectarines are a great substitute for peaches, or consider a combination of both.

# Resources

## Recommended Pressure Cookers

Fagor Chef Pressure Cooker (expensive, but I love it!)

Fagor 2-by-1 Splendid 5-Piece Pressure Cooker Set

Presto 4-Quart (3.8 L) Stainless Steel Pressure Cooker

Presto 01365 6-Quart (5.8 L) Stainless Steel Pressure Cooker, Deluxe

Presto 307912 6-Quart (5.8 L) Stainless Steel Pressure Cooker

## Recommended Books

*Great Vegetarian Cooking Under Pressure*, Lorna Sass

*The New Fast Food: The Veggie Queen Pressure Cooks Whole Food Meals in Less Than 30 Minutes*, Jill Nussinow, MS, RD

## Recommended Websites

www.hippressurecooking.com
www.jlgoesvegan.com
www.veganpressurecooking.com
www.theveggiequeen.com

## Recommended Classes

Author JL Fields offers pressure cooking classes in Colorado Springs and the surrounding area (visit www.govegan withjl.com).

# Acknowledgments

**It was a privilege to work with the enthusiastic and encouraging** team at Fairwinds Press. Special thanks to Amanda Waddell for being a thoughtful and patient editor, and to project manager Betsy Gammons, art director Heather Godin, book designer Amanda Richmond, and publisher Winnie Prentiss. Thank you for putting great vegan content out into the world.

Brilliantly talented Kate Lewis, thank you for turning my recipes into works of art through your photos.

Heartfelt thanks to my agent Angela Miller, who inherited me on a previous project and kept me for this, and future projects. I am grateful for your support and encouragement.

My recipe testers—several of whom had never touched a pressure cooker prior to this project—are my heroes! My thanks to Ashley Flitter, Barb Musick, Barbara Ravid, Ben Covington, Bonnie Hildebrand, Carolina Meyer, Cat DiStasio, Connie Maschan, Jared Bigman, Kathleen Graas, Kavitha Selvaraj, Lauren Collier, Laurie Morrison, Linda Lauder, Lisa Poveda, Liz Dee, Marcia Kalisch, Marti Miller Hall, Melissa McPherson, Shannon Kinsella, Vegan Mos (Michael Suchman and Ethan Ciment), Wendy Moniuk, and Whitney Ferdon.

Ginny Messina and Victoria Moran: I can never thank you enough for walking beside me as friends, mentors, and colleagues. Thank you for your unwavering commitment to the animals.

I am privileged to lead the Colorado Springs Vegan & Vegetarian Group and am so incredibly thankful to each and every member for embracing me when I became a Coloradan.

I am humbled and devoted to my blog readers. Always.

Mom, dad, and my sisters—thank you for never being surprised by what I do.

To my husband Dave, thank you for being my biggest supporter, for being open to a veg journey, and for being the best cat daddy ever to CK and Ernie.

Going vegan changed my life. I wish for a world free of harm and cruelty to every single being. That's why I create vegan recipes—for the animals.

# About the Author

**JL Fields is a vegan cook, lifestyle coach, educator, and co-author** of *Vegan for Her: The Woman's Guide to Being Healthy and Fit on a Plant-Based Diet* (Da Capo Press, 2013). She was also a contributor to *Running, Thinking, Eating: A Vegan Anthology* and writes for both the *Colorado Springs Gazette* and the *Colorado Springs Independent*.

A devoted culinary student, JL has studied at the Natural Gourmet Institute, and completed the Intensive Study Program at the Christina Pirello School of Natural Cooking and Integrative Health Studies. To find out more about JL's classes, speaking engagements, and more, visit her at www.goveganwithjl.com.

# About the Photographer

**Kate Lewis is a New York City– and Ohio–based food and travel** photographer and stylist. Over the years, she has held every restaurant position from hostess, server, and bartender to chocolatier, barista, and chef. Her culinary background and fine art training combined with her passion for food prompted her to begin shooting portraits for renowned chefs and highly-stylized photographs. Kate's photography and styling has worked with national publications like *Food & Wine*, *VegNews*, and more than ten cookbooks. Follow Kate's everyday adventures on Instagram and Twitter @_Kate_Lewis.

# Index